Our Journey Through the Seasons

Jerry S. Barry

CONTENTS

Dedication   vii
Acknowledgments   viii
THE JOURNEY   11
SPRING   15
THE SPRING REST STOP   21
    The Rest Stop Defined   30
    Stragglers   35
    Predators   35
    The Distracted   36
    The Mendicants   37
    The Hoarders   37
    The Entrepreneurs   38
    The Entertainers   39
    The Spenders   30
    The Dreamers   41
    The Peddlers   42
THE STORMY WEATHER   43
SUMMER (THE TRANSITION)   49
THE JOURNEY   54
    Compromises   57
    The Lanes of Traffic   60
THE SUMMER REST STOP   63
    Aspirations   66
    Responsibilities   67
A PARTNER OR PASSENGER   71
    Responsibilities to The Self   79
    Qualities of A Good Working Partner   82
ONTO THE HIGHWAY TOWARDS FALL   88
    Rejoining the Highway Toward Autumn   90
    Internal Distractions   93
    Learning to Look as We Travel 96
    Beauty and Ugliness   98

The Culture of Ugliness	101
The Products of Ugliness	103
Ugly Politics of Survival	104
Elements of Distraction	105
The War of Opposites	108
Extended Egotism	110
Nurturing the Philosophy of Opposites	115
Spoils of The War of Opposites	118
The War Intensifies	120
Counter Offensives	123
The City of Paradoxia	127
Benefits of the Storm	130
Animal Response to the Storm	133
Human Responses to the Storm	136
The Storm Within a Relationship	139
View to the Back Seat	143
Defining Love in the Journey of Parenthood	147
WINTER – THE REST STOP	153
The Hazards of Loving	154
Finding Ourselves Again	157
The Possible Virtue of a Crisis	161
Finding Back Ourselves	165
Attributes of the Spirit	169
Internal and External	170
Freedom and the Act of Will	172
WINTER	179
Winter Illusions	181
Misinterpretations	185
The Peculiar and the Rudimentary	187
The Ego and the Spirit	190
Living in the Spirit	193
Hazards of Winter Travel	197
Missions, Purposes and Entrapments	199
Enemies in the Journey of Life	202

The Positive Effect of the Negative 205
The Philosophy of Opposites in Winter 209
Retribution: Life Produces It Like a Work of
Art 212
THE WINTER REST STOP 217
Travelling by Intuition 219
Maintaining Our Focus in Winter 222
The Bipolar Nature of the Life We Live 227
Stragglers 231
How Travelers Become Stragglers 234
Hypocrites 236
The Universal Will Versus Physical Power 237
The Futility of Self-Aggrandizement 240
EXIT FROM THE WINTER REST STOP 245
What Winter Travel Means 248
BEYOND THE HORIZON 253
THE CONCLUSION:
CLUES TO THE SYMBOLS OF TRAVEL 255
The Challenge 255
The Paradox of Life Is the Shape You Give to
It 258
LIFE'S LIVING QUESTIONS 259
ABOUT THE AUTHOR 261

Jerry S. Barry

DEDICATION

To my friend Everette McKenzie who finished her
journey too early and missed the joy of reading this
book.

Jerry S. Barry

ACKNOWLEDGMENTS

The Rev. Dr. Beverly Coker challenged me to take this trip to see what I will find along the way.

Rachel Mc Gregor survived my scribbles and Vangella Buchanan's creative input made my material presentable

Dr. Jacqueline Evans Phillip, my coach, has encouraged me and showed patience.

My friend, Donovan Haughton, has never been tired of my endless ramblings about the subject of this book

My wife, Gwen, encouraged me to test my ideas as they developed

MY THANKS TO ALL OF YOU!

Jerry S. Barry

There is no such thing as an accident on the highway of life

THE JOURNEY

We have all lived in seasons, in the long term or in the short term, whether or not we have come to acknowledge or appreciate them. We may have entered our current season from different points and perspectives, perhaps even with the option to choose our path, if we have been so gifted or predisposed. Our path may have been also predetermined by circumstance or a special calling that was beyond our control.

If we were able to figure out our life's probabilities, then it might not be worth making the journey; for we would understand why we entered this journey in the first place. Since this always seems to be beyond our comprehension, the best we can do is to focus on keeping to our path according to the nature of the traffic and the virtue of the terrain on which we have been privileged to navigate. Diversion may be a pleasant part of travel, since it makes our journey richer and more exciting; but it also helps us to stay alert for bumps along the way.

Sometimes, the road is crowded with other travelers going in the same direction. We need to be alert for the brake-lights ahead of us and for others' poor driving habits, for the responsibility will be ours for any collision along our path. We may even have to account for any casualties that we have indirectly caused, and to compensate for wreckages we might leave behind. The only insurance is what we possess in our hearts to give to others, in gratitude for what we have received.

There is no such thing as an accident
on the highways of life, even when
our exit seems to come too suddenly
upon us.

We control the destiny of our travels through the choices that we make and the intersections that we take. We all journey on the road to perfection, although some of us may get distracted or even lost along the way. There is one thing that we do have to be very careful about, and that is what we decide to do during our rest stops. We must not let ourselves get too complacent, or fall asleep for too long, for we may lose our sense of direction. A whole life's journey could be wasted if we try to back in the direction from which we came, while the true purpose of our journey still awaits us with an urgency to fill that void.

Jerry S. Barry

Spring! When everything is new and fresh

SPRING

Spring is a time of freedom, when everything is new and fresh, even though it is reborn of the old and grounded in the customs and crude familiarity that possessed our past. When nature begins to rejuvenate and the issues of life spring forth in our minds, we should be able to blossom like the lilies and the roses to show the true colors of what we are supposed to be. It is also the season of youth when the wind blows with excitement and high anticipation. Every vein of our youth tells us that the world is wonderful and full of unlimited enjoyment, and that everyone and everything exists to fulfill our aspirations.

Those of us in the spring of our youth are forever seeking new adventures that follow our fantasies and dreams of how we view the world. When we are in the infancy of our existence, there is a tendency to be very egotistic in order to fulfill our every need. Ideas are always sprouting from our beings, especially when we are in the spring state of our minds. Possibilities are endless in our puerile minds and the energy is boundless. It is a time to sing and dance and play. We come into life with this natural enthusiasm to prepare ourselves for greater things to come. Hopefully, we can or will get the rhythm and reasoning right to graduate to the aspirations of our true purpose, and not just what we have become through circumstances.

The lane that we have merged into in the highway of our lives will have its own potholes and obstacles around which we will have to navigate at our discretion.

We may be born into special privileges which we may take for granted, but they may not necessarily be ours by right, even if we have grown accustomed to being showered with them by those around us. We may blossom in our lifestyle so much that we may come to deserve these privileges, but when we build our expectations upon them, we can create potholes in our travels that may be more than we can manage. We may even become so preoccupied with those expectations that we may not be able to detect the potholes in the path before us.

Some, however, have the inherent ability to

Potholes on the journey

manage on their own. They have the eye to discern the potholes, bumps, and other distractions, and have cushions to absorb the shocks. Any distractions become chapters in the lesson of life they use to inspire those who are less endowed. It is never too early to learn how to steer and maneuver in the highway of life.

Those formative years of Spring present the best opportunities for us to find ourselves and our way in navigating through the challenges of this world. When our minds are at that elementary stage, we can grapple at big things in little bites, to make it easier for our little minds to digest our true purpose.

Sometimes, we need a partner or a role model to facilitate the experience that ignites us on our way to finding ourselves. He or she will not have the key, but can lead us to where we can find it in ourselves. We all exist with the key to our own glory; it is just that we need first to find it. Some of us have missed the key because we have run too fast through our Spring season. Some of us may have been driving on the edge, taking all the risks that are common at this age, and losing ourselves and our way in the process.

Instead of basking in the joys and eccentricities of the present era of our growth, there are some who extend beyond the capabilities of their age in order to conform to the expectations of an illusion given to them, and have subsequently run out of stamina too soon for their age.

Spring is the season of our innocence when we can find joy in everything. Even the non-living takes on a life of its own nature, perpetuating a spiritual quality or behavioral tendency that is not a usual part of its being. It is through the world of fantasy that we create a reality of our own that will serve us for years to come.

The speculative adventures from the inner corners of our mind become the cornerstones we use to create the ideal world of our hidden aspirations. That is when we find it feasible and even invigorating to talk to the flora and fauna, creating chains of adventures in our own unique heaven. If we could only include real people in this world, our heaven would feel complete and real; but then our highway would be too crowded with people changing lanes to align with their aspirations; and our journey would be plagued with the brake-lights of travelers struggling to avoid collision. When the journey gets this crowded, it is easy to get lost in our egocentric tendencies, by not recognizing the congestion for what it is worth, risking head-on collisions, or even wearing ourselves out emotionally and spiritually to try to avoid them.

However, there are those in this season who have already become exhausted from living on the edge, and who have been recycled into manure for those that are better equipped or cultured for the race. They have lost any incentive to reach out for resources or comfort, that would help to rejuvenate themselves. They retreat into the darkness, into territories that make no demand on their honesty, fruitfulness, and integrity. Spring is not the season to be hibernating or indulging in slothfulness simply because it is convenient, pleasurable, and self-assuring to do so.

Some of us are in a perpetual state of hibernation that depends on the generosity of those more industrious to excuse our lack of awareness, instead providing basic resources from their own talent. Those in this type of supported hibernation never seem able to hear the birds chirping at sunrise, nor smell the lilies in bloom. The waters of the brook may try desperately to play hide and seek with our ears, demanding our attention as they clear a path down the rocks to settle in quiet ripples in the pool below. How easy it is to miss the liquid diamond of our souls flowing with a song of hope and peace. We cannot hear, except but to drink and quench our physical thirst, spill what is left and walk away.

Some of us never truly recover from the trauma, and may stall our engines or endure a flat, while others suffer a collapse of their whole world and need a tow truck to take them from one exit to the next.

THE SPRING REST STOP

The rest stop is a necessary part of our journey, if we are able to recognize it for all its benefits, entrapments and illusions. It all begins with the choice we make, and the state of our mind in which we make that choice. The need for a rest stop must not be influenced mainly by circumstances beyond our control which force us to stop through desperation. The choice must be separated from the need, so that our vision is clear, instead of making our selection from the mirages of desperation.

If we allow ourselves to get too thirsty in the desert areas, we can interpret lurking quicksand for a lush waterfall.

It is all a mirage from the fever that results from the constant overdrives and wear and tear that requires a brief period of adjustment. A quick glance on the dashboard would suffice as a good habit, even if our car is new and we are in this early phase of our journey. Even new cars suffer from metal fatigue and their cooling systems are only doing their first test run, so we do not want to take too much for granted based on our confidence in what we had been told. Even so, stopping for an opportunity to stretch and give our system a chance to rejuvenate may prove to be more valuable than we think for the next stage of the journey. That glance to the dashboard is the reminder to keep in touch with our sense of purpose and mission and not get too engrossed in enjoying the journey because the road was smooth and new, or preoccupied with proving ourselves worthy of the challenges that we face.

We are not on this trip only for the sake of the journey, but for the value of ourselves that we are bringing to the world. What we have nurtured may seem small and insignificant in contrast to what is out there, but there is no need to pretend that we are bigger than we are if what we bring can multiply in magic proportions in the lives of everyone with whom we come in touch. That is why we need to stop and refresh ourselves to keep alert to the valuable cargo that we carry, and not let thieves get the opportunity to plunder our merchandise when we lay prostrate in a state of exhaustion or temporary unconsciousness.

What about our fuel gauge after we have exhausted our philosophy to the limits of our understanding at this phase of our growth and perception? Do we have to experience a stall in the emergency lane of our existence to remind ourselves that we should have checked our fuel capacity? Taking quick naps in the middle of traffic is obviously not a good tactic to adopt, or this whole journey of life would not be worth it in the first place. The manner in which we choose our rest stops can create hazards for other motorists confidently speeding on their

way.

Even changing your lanes in the process has to do with calculated precision and utmost consideration for others. First of all, there are those who have adopted you as the mentor of their lives and are content to drive behind you. Even in youth, you can be a source of utmost inspiration to young and old alike, but you must give them enough to go on their own, or they will follow you to the rest stop.

There are different kinds of followers, at various levels of maturity and sophistication. Since you must maintain your focus on what is ahead, you should be content to leave them to accommodate their own needs as they see fit; however, it is courteous to do it in an orderly and appropriate manner. Some of them may have never learned to adopt a philosophy of their own, or create a challenge worthy of their ability and talent. They are the complacent types who are content to be copycats, leeching off of people who seem to be headed in their direction. Their change of events and directions are dictated by those they allow to dominate them. They are pained by their own inner convictions, unless those convictions are sanctioned by the words and actions of celebrities, famous heroes or even social rejects possessing strong will power. They are easily scooped up into all kinds of scams and movements and tend to park in the tents of cults. It is only through good fortune that they may find themselves linked to people with good intentions, otherwise they could end up as one of the casualties you may pass along the highway, accidents that create gridlocks we all will have to endure.

There are those who follow us in order to reap the material or spiritual benefits we attract, to their own advantage. First, there is the material gain of plagiarizing someone else's ideas to market them as merchandise in attractive packages on shelves for curious customers to consume. They loot whatever scraps you may discard into the garbage or manage to let slip from your possession, or out of your mouth. Some are chronic panhandlers who will perpetually use the best of their talents to devise ways to benefit from the generosity of others.

They are not exactly social parasites, but persons of goodwill and talent who have made poor choices regarding the purpose and function of their lives.

There are those, however, who may follow you for the mutual satisfaction of validating their intelligence, and to boost their self-confidence to confirm that their pursuits are genuinely their own. These are harder to get rid of because they need others, including you, to give them a sense of direction. They are forever parked next to you, engaging you in circular arguments and discussions for the purpose of attracting attention to themselves at your expense. If you do not become aware of these types early enough, they can entrap you into their futile missions of intellectual perambulations. For them, the greatest benefit of a rest stop is to puff out a great quantity of smoke to boast the quality of their cigar to other smokers like themselves.

You, on the other hand, will need clean wholesome air to revitalize your lungs for the next phase of your pursuits, and not get submerged in the sea of pollution engineered by conceited malcontents. Even they need your help, however, to rescue themselves from their addiction to partaking in these intellectual escapades. These mindless pursuits make up for the lack of moral convictions and real intellectual substance that would otherwise support their repressed philosophy. Perhaps you should take the time to help point them in the direction of self-sufficiency so that they do not waste valuable initiatives for a worthy cause waiting around to profit from your mistakes.

Those who feel they have missed their rest stop may actually not have even reached it yet. What they have actually missed are the joys and eccentricities of childhood because they were getting entangled with the priorities of the adult world. How else would they find themselves blossoming into the vibrancy of youth, but getting stuck with the quest of the status quo, the pursuit of wealth and fame, and the stench of prejudice, raw aggression and abuse of power?

This kind of culture requires that we never use a rest stop, even if it necessitates spewing oil on others along the way, all the better to make a slippery path for all who choose to follow. That is an exit that the arrogant and the ignorant always take instead of a rest stop. The functions of a rest stop are so alien to their ambitions, that they deliberately avoid it at all costs to conform to the demands of excess, power and self-aggrandizement. They will never have any other choice because their GPS-es are programmed to go nowhere beyond that exit. There they share lanes with dictators, shrewd and ruthless politicians, public leaders and even despots.

The paradigm for setting values here starts from the bottom, and the more drivers we force out of their lanes the better. The highway is always strewn with debris from the fate of innocent lives destroyed by the ambitions of the rich, the bigots, and the morally and spiritually deficient in society.

Their territory is populated by the machinery of juggernauts that consume the mass of innocents and simple minded, and produce heroes out of thieves and vagabonds.

Ruthless competition is the way of life here, where the importance and status of people are determined by how well they oil the machinery of monetary profits. In this world of opposites, even education and morality become subservient to the principle of power. Might determines what is right and everyone and everything is dispensable except for those who have reached the top.

Schools become grooming institutions in the art of survival to compete for the status quo, where even parents help to bend the rules to transform ordinary tools of learning into destructive weapons of thought for the upliftment of the family.

The journey here is only up to the mountain top where the lane gets narrower and emptier. Rest stops never come, only the pinnacle where the victor balances precariously, with no chance for a return. Those who awaken to the predicament of their lives want to turn back, even for their children's sake, but they cannot back down from the pinnacle of their pursuits.

There is not enough room at a pinnacle to even turn much less to maneuver and detour. The pinnacle of power and wealth is in airtight compartments balancing precariously in the wind of circumstances. Its fatal enemy is change of any sort, and it is even more fatal to get stuck or blackmailed to hold your ground where there is not enough room to even stand, while you suffer in silence, heart heavy with regrets, and you facing nothing but an empty sky that spells your fate.

Those of us who are not distracted by illusions and make it to our rest stop, still have to make full use of the time we spend. A rest stop can present its own share of attractions and distractions that can distort the true nature of its benefits.

The pinnacle of power and wealth is in airtight compartments

We take a rest stop to relax, recuperate, and rejuvenate both our machinery and ourselves. This is when we are able to examine the internal workings of our system through introspection, speculation, and analysis.

We reflect on the nature of our impact on others, and the impact of our commitment to our beliefs and self-convictions. That is why we take leisure in deflecting the tension of our minds through seemingly non-objective pursuits of pleasure. We can play a game of tennis in our minds of the possibilities, the pros and cons of our actions, our decisions or our state of mind. Our objective is not to win, or to narrow our focus away from the wider paradigms of wisdom. We do not seek a conclusion, but rather to give some closure to what we are trying to seek. Wisdom is infinite and boundless, in stark contrast to what the pinnacle that power and wealth amounts to. Its domains unfold into boundless horizons, each beyond its own sunrise of enlightenment.

We need no skills nor proficiencies to navigate the domains governed by love, only the appropriate state of mind to be our compass. It does not matter whether we pray or meditate, sing or dance, go on vacation or sit in our backyard, read or write, sculpt or paint to awaken our inner being to this state of mind. The ecstasy can even be in the travel, the process of getting there, just the act of heading in that direction.

Every mile of every day brings its
own fulfillments with
anticipation of greater things yet
to come.

THE REST STOP DEFINED

The rest stop is like a charging station where we take a deep breath with our psyche to delve into another dimension of the wisdom that we seek. This is why we must pause before our rest stop to get rid of any excess cling-ons and redundancies, perhaps by visiting a car wash to rinse our system of dust, acid rain, and other hazards to the conveniences of travel. It is important to let our feet touch the ground so that we learn how to listen; not merely to hear what people are saying, but what they are trying to say subliminally. This is one way in which we can give life to things that would otherwise be left for dead.

During our lighter moments at the rest stop, we need to guard ourselves against getting lost in ingesting the niceties available. Some of the items on attraction are for the consumption of travelers of a different appetite, whose lifestyle and general makeup can tolerate or even thrive on this kind of nourishment. We do not need to encumber ourselves and our system with additional weight and unnecessary clutter. There are items and issues that may seem lively and relative, but in context are much more connected to the dead than to the living. Why would we choose to dabble with such items prior to continuing our precious journey, or even take them or their influence with us? We should even be wary to ingest certain snacks that have the potential to make our feet or eyes heavy, or provoke our system into a multitude of reactions.

While it has been said that a man is what he eats, it should better be understood that a man is also what he decides to eat, since our decisions come before our actions. We should embrace the habit of analyzing our decisions before we act on them, so that we burden ourselves less with the ritual of confessing and asking for forgiveness for actions that are part of our intentions.

Some actions have the potential to be lethal to our very intentions, our aspirations or our very philosophy of life, and may even render us incapable or incompetent to make the trip altogether. Why would we come this far to abandon our whole journey at a rest stop? It would be easy if we forgot where we were going because we were too busy entertaining ourselves with toys and distractions. Toys and persons that give temporary pleasure have no journey to make, or glorious aspirations to fulfill.

The rest stop is the beginning and the end of their mission or aspiration, and your engagement with them is the fulfillment of their very existence. Either you have raised their pedigree that high or you have lowered yourself many times below to make a horrible understatement of what you have become. Two gulps of alcohol can render you incapable of standing steadily on your feet, much less focus to hold to your lane on the highway.

Cheap pleasures can make themselves perfect substitutes for the higher objectives in life, so much to the extent that some travelers abandon their trip altogether to become gullible consumers, going from one rest stop to another only to seek out the variety. If you see the rest stop more overcrowded than usual, take a quick glance at the number of derelicts panhandling in the parking lot. They are all staying at the rest stop to enjoy it more thoroughly than they should.

Our environment often speaks to us in tangible ways loud and clear, if we only have the ears to hear and the eyes to see.

Most rest stops look alike in their physical structures and layout. There are spacious parking lots with many parking spaces, booths that sell useful and silly trinkets, fast food stalls and some space for dining, gaming, and watching television. They are all designed to suit the travelers and cater to their needs. However, each rest stop is unique according to the priorities of the season in which it is located. The Winter rest stop is a little cozier and indoors, lots of lights to buffer the bleak outside and very warm inside, for obvious reasons. Spring and summer are more outdoor oriented as people dress to sunbathe even with their clothes on.

What makes each rest stop unique to a traveler is the kinds of people he encounters and the kinds of experiences he shares with them. We all gravitate to the kind of people who are the very reflection of ourselves. We search for ourselves in other people when we meet, and will never be disappointed to find our kind at each rest stop as we go. There is something about our human magnetism that enables us to know and find our own and for them to find us. We may not always want to admit or accept that internal pull in our natures or the parking lot, and we know that they will follow us secretly and we finally meet and say our first hello.

There is absolutely nothing wrong with socializing with other travelers like our ourselves, provided we do not forget that we are in transit and have a journey to make. When the person who we meet becomes more important than the journey then we know that it is not the rest stop to be blamed, but that we have come all this way on the journey to find ourselves. Most people at the rest stop have graduated from their journey and are stuck there. All they need is company and their aspirations are fulfilled. When they approach you as you arrive, they are looking for themselves in you. All they need is your validation or some clue that you are one of them. They are all detractors or distractors whose mission is to take you off your true purpose and make your trip to join them in defecting from your travel as they have done. Perhaps we can explore some of them and their characteristic and discover how our usefulness to them far surmounts their usefulness to us. They are all stragglers in some way or the other, but some are more invested in their obsession than in the straggling itself.

Some people at the rest stop

STRAGGLERS

These are the real chronic stragglers whose obsession is just being free of any obligation or commitment to anything. They have no journey to make, so they have nowhere to go. The rest stop is their home where they hide away from themselves. They go around in circles, recycling themselves with junk ideas they have picked up to give themselves something to do. They operate against the dictates of the growth changes in their body and mind. They are not only unwilling but are adamantly opposed to moving on and respond to the obligations and demands of their growth. Change is their enemy and growth is their pain. They are stuck in limbo and may never be able to live their lives fully. Stragglers are excellent complainers. They sit around impressively on the verge of homelessness, and complain that they are being abandoned, neglected and rejected, when it is they who are doing that to themselves. They can tell you what is wrong about everything but never what is right about anything.

PREDATORS

There are those who make it their mission to detour anyone or anything worthwhile to feed their lust for cheap fulfillment. They are ravenous and desperate to do anything to survive at the cost of others, especially the weak, the gullible, and the innocent. They destroy the character and integrity of unknown heroes in their community, desecrate shrines of great ideas and concepts of honor. They put on all their various disguises of sincerity and honesty so that they can be allowed to prowl freely in the territory and private spaces of their potential victims. Their strategy is to strike their victims at the most vulnerable moment in their lives, when their victims would have trusted them most. Predators employ vices to entrap and destroy virtues with intrigues that are beyond the anticipation or comprehension of their victims, serving as baits to entice their victims to bite.

THE DISTRACTED

These travelers are temporarily disoriented and preoccupied with sensation and material and spiritual trinkets. When we do not have a real sound reason and purpose to travel, the sense of urgency is never there to reach a destination. Distracted travelers never really figured out where they were going, so they get attracted to every little thing that gets their attention. The rest stop is perhaps the most suitable place for distracted travelers, since they are potential hazard on a speeding highway and may cause serious accidents with their attitude of shallow commitment to their travel. They have a short attention span and are likely to change lanes haphazardly, causing great inconvenience to serious travelers. They love entertainment of every kind and would sample every stall or booth and whatever it has to offer. When we do not want to see where we are going, we do not bother ourselves to look.

THE MENDICANTS

Those suffering from a chronic lack of ideas do not know what to do with ideas, even when valuable ideas are given to them. They are the ones who make litter of ideas and ideas of life, but are constantly begging for new and fresher ones. They travel without maps so they can ask for directions, and are always asking for advice to which they will pay no heed. At the rest stop, they will discover what they really need and then they will realize they have no money to buy. Mendicants love to live off the generosity and good nature of their victims, depriving them of things they can acquire for themselves. They exhibit all the postures and attitudes of pity and dependency as if they had never really prepared for travel. These are life's travelers whose main purpose or motivation is to beg their way through travel, unloading their responsibilities and commitments to anyone willing and able to oblige them.

THE HOARDERS

These travelers suffer from a chronic addiction of selfishness and egotism. Their insular way of thinking makes them more efficient at grasping and collecting more than they need, until their vehicle is cluttered with irrelevancy and redundancy of every kind. They compile leftovers of every issue or circumstance to gain the attention of those around them. They carry their luggage of overused or discarded ideas with them everywhere they go. Even at the rest stop, when they should be relaxing their minds to rejuvenate, they carry around their valuables in large bags and haversacks, and on their faces. Hoarders never give of themselves and their resources because they can hardly ever afford to do so. They are too preoccupied with devising ways of getting more of what they do not need or will never be able to use. Their purpose of travel in life is to collect and compile as much as they can get, even when it overburdens their vehicle and discomforts their travel.

THE ENTREPRENEURS

For these people, the purpose of life is strictly to do business. They are usually very focused in their endeavors and can perform acrobatic stunts doing business while going full speed on the highway of life. At the rest stop, they can be money lenders to capture the resources of less vigilant travelers, or they can be collectors looking for value in things, events, and people. For them, anything can be of value, or they invest value into it so that it can qualify for them to do business with it. Their whole life is worth nothing more than engaging in their kind of business, and the rest stop for them is just another territory to exploit and rampage. Such people are too busy doing business to observe the sun rising in the morning or setting in the evening. They travel at great speed to get ahead of the competition, and never rest at the rest stop while there is business to be done.

THE ENTERTAINERS

These are the specially talented who can do tricks and performances to impress others about the life they can only portray on stage but will never be able to live. They are good actors who get so invested in their mandates and performances that they forget who they are. The pleasure of their fans and audiences is their mission in life and that is what gives meaning and purpose in everything they do. Their fans dictate their desires and aspirations and their performances are the measures of their fulfillment. Entertainers go on journeys in their imagination into the world of fantasy that they are loved by their fans. It may be good for their sanity for them to think that way, for they will be too devastated to learn that their fans simply use them for convenience to service their own needs. Some travelers even deceive themselves emulating the qualities of these glorified absent-minded schizophrenics, assuming that to be like them is equivalent to making their own life's journey through.

THE SPENDERS

For these travelers, life is all about having a good time getting and doing what they want. Spending is their notion of prestige and satisfaction, and they will do everything to impress those who both admire and benefit from their obsession. The only problem they have is spending money and consuming resources that they do not possess. They pride themselves in taking prerogative with ideas and conclusions that are not their own. They tend to go bankrupt for lack of ideas, since they never really invested in any of value. Spenders look glamorous and can make great speeches and proclamations on issues that do not concern them, because they did not experience or never understood them. They can be seen in the front lines of demonstrations, festivals and parades, celebrating other people's conflicts and happiness. Owners of stalls and booths at the rest stop rely on their aimless spending to keep their businesses afloat and thriving. The spending is infused into their appetite to the extent that is surpasses being an obsession and is now their emotional state of happiness. They are among the victims of the philosophy of opposite, who straggle along the journey of life and never get past the first rest stop.

While we are trapped in our vices and selfish desires, we cease to recognize much less enjoy the true benefits of life and living.

A blind or distracted driver is a hazard to himself and other travelers, since he is already off the road even as he is traveling on it.

THE DREAMERS

These are travelers who descend from the highway looking weary, sleepy, and tired of the realities of life. They dream and hope for a better way of life, but remain stuck and dedicated to the one they are living. Dreamers have lofty ideas of how the world can be fixed, and they tend to boost their self-esteem with aspirations that do not belong to them. They have this unique quality of solving the world's problems by speculating and philosophizing on the peripheries of the issues and avoiding the core altogether. They may even have vacated the highway to abscond from the responsibilities of travelling. At the rest stop, they can sing great carols of hope and perform illustrious poems of victory and mechanical advancement. After they have done what they think is their portion of the performance, they will settle to finally do what they do best and dream

41

their lives away.

THE PEDDLERS

Unlike the entrepreneurs, peddlers settle for the crumbs to do business and run their lives. All the recycled ideas and issues can be repackaged in flamboyant colors to become shiny trinkets in the forefront of their booths and aspirations. They are always busy turning little nothings into something to give themselves something to do. They walk around intently to even become the booths from which they sell their trinkets dangling from their hands and bodies. Ordinary travelers at the rest stop will not care, but the peddlers succeed in arousing their curiosity in what they have to sell.

When we are at a rest stop and have nothing to do, even nothing can become something when someone stands behind it. Peddlers display their own breed of courage in the manner they respond to life's challenges. Even the little things can mean a lot to give our lives some purpose and direction. Perhaps we can start with the little simple things, if the complicated ones are too big for us.

When you are traveling the course of this life, you need to be ready for the unpredictable

THE STORMY WEATHER

Every season brings with it certain adjustments of climatic conditions that are necessary, although they may not always suit our understanding or satisfaction. The same season that brings us the flowers, the rain, the birds, the rabbits and the butterflies, brings us the hurricanes, the tornadoes, the floods and the mudslides. It is just nature taking its course and fulfilling its obligations to us and the earth.

Nature is universal and holds no petty grievances or vendettas of a personal nature toward place, man, or beast.

It achieves balance where and when it is due in accordance to the needs and conditions present. This is how and why we can predict weather by observing related conditions that are likely to bring about the same results.

If this fails, we can assume that there must have been conditions that were beyond our observation or comprehension, and that we should humbly accept the deliberations of nature over and above our narrow speculation. A man who challenges the deliberations of nature has indirectly exposed his lack of constraint and understanding. He who goes further to ridicule and judge the performance of nature is hopelessly ignorant and egotistic. If we have not yet reduced ourselves that low, we should at least prepare for ourselves an umbrella or a raincoat and boots, and keep on the lookout for the weather forecast.

When you are traveling the course of this life, regardless of the season, you need to be alert and ready for the unpredictable, the unexpected or the unusual. Life does not come with an instruction manual to tell us what to expect when or where; for if it did, we would degenerate to becoming imbeciles, bored out of our wits.

To wish you had known what was coming is to encourage this habit of thinking, which gets cancerous and pervades every kind of activity in our lives. Already technology has brought us ridiculously close to predicting the weather to the last detail and we are certain we know how to manage the confidence we have acquired. Technology, with all its academic and intellectual prowess is hardly able to predict the precise course of human thought and action that will influence the social and political events in the course of history. We are all at the mercy of this kind of climate, and can only wait to respond when it rains or pours. That, however, is not wholly as true as it sounds.

The predictability of matters on human affairs can be measured by the actions of every one of us. When, collectively, we send the ethers of our attitudes and our actions up into the atmosphere of social and political affairs, there is bound to be an appropriate and reciprocal reaction in reverse to bring about the balance that is necessary.

Much like water finding its own level, everything always finds its own balance consequently, very often when we least expect it. Human beings are often so preoccupied with the selfish gratification of their actions that they are never ready for the consequences. However, whether we acknowledge them or not, the energy of all our actions, decisions, or intentions continue to permeate the atmosphere and the psyches of those around us. With the internet and social media, they continue to spread at the speed of light to the far ends of the universe, to resonate with force and precision that are quite remarkable and often unpredictable.

We contribute to this energy in more ways than we can suspect. First of all, the actions that have been generated from our personalities become the catalysts that affect the lives of those with whom we come into contact, especially those who depend on us to charge their batteries in the course of their travel. We can get so egocentric in our focus that everything and everyone around us ceases to be real except for when it serves our own self-interest.

People, therefore, can become expendable, processed in our minds like furniture, utensils, or consumables as we sincerely go about our business as usual to chart our way to the fulfillment of our dreams.

Subconsciously, and sometimes deliberately, we engineer the climate that wires itself down the network, up and down the grid of the social ladder of our community, and things begin to happen.

When the rain begins to fall and everyone starts to get wet, we may be able to grab our umbrellas, but we can hardly ignore the thunder and lightning as they get louder and more aggressive. When the storms begin to sweep down upon us all, and we know not where we are going or coming from, then we get concerned about our own safety and find ourselves forced to pretend that we are concerned for others as well.

The season of Spring offers us a feasible excuse to cover our youth and immaturity; so we give ourselves the license to saturate our conscience freely with our guilt, only to try to appeal for redemption and forgiveness later.

When, in the name of business, politics, and practicality we contribute to the climate of hate, repression, exploitation and crime, we may try to cool our consciences by doing charity work and making lofty speeches to align our integrity with the opposites of our action. When, in the name of religion and goodwill, we may indulge in all shades of hypocrisy and falsehoods under the pretext of serving God and humanity, but then go to the mountaintop for redemption to quote the scriptures and pray with sincerity for all to see and hear. The more it appears that we are succeeding in penetrating the ozone layers of the world with our misdeeds, the more reckless we can get in our appetite to continue.

It is easy then to be blind to injustice, prejudice, and corruption, and to prostitute the virtues of good to create benefits and access for harbingers of evil. When we feel the rumble of the earthquake and suspect that the tsunami is headed our way, we often hurry from our rest stop, leaving others behind to deal with the destruction we have caused.

SUMMER (THE TRANSITION)

Summer comes very subtly upon us, as we graduate across its borders into what looks like familiar territory. The sun still shines as brightly as

The heat of the summer season can induce illusions

it did in Spring, but only hotter. The wind seems to be conveniently moody, blowing when it wants to and getting too humid and stationary when we want it to do otherwise. Summer can deceive us into believing that we are having or pursuing fun when we are actually just responding to the conditions around us and taking advantage of the opportunities that keep emerging before us.

This is the phase in our lives where we become bombarded with multiple conceptions of what fun means. The most misleading of these concepts is the one that confines ideas of fun to this domain because of the incidental amenities that come with it. Most of us go to the beach or to a picnic, not just because we want to, but also because we have to. Being outdoors in the water or under the shade are ways that we can beat the heat. This 'beat the heat' syndrome has made us hypochondriacs in our perception about our normal affairs in life that we associate most of our other functions as stressful, boring, or even traumatic. When we persuade ourselves that we are happy because it is Summer, then we are indirectly convincing ourselves that we are likely to be unhappy when it is not Summer.

The journey of this life and any other can and will be whatever we convince ourselves it is in our minds, before we even embark on it. The heat of the summer season can induce illusions that we can adopt as reality, steering our lives into different directions in pursuit of them. Fresh out of Spring, we may not have the experience or the seasoned judgment to even suspect much less question a mirage that is before us. When still full of fantasy, our minds are more prone to the illusions of the heat of Summer. Much of what seems real is so because we become so thirsty to fulfill our aspirations, we may rush to a pool of quicksand to drink, or head to a waterfall over a cliff.

When we cross the border into Summer, we need to recognize that we are still influenced by Spring, and much of the rationale that comes with it into this new territory.

If our rationale for negotiating the traffic ahead of us is based purely on what we had succeeded with doing in the past, then our limitations will actually be increasing without us being fully aware of it. The worst of all realizations are the ones that come too late, when the tools we are attempting to use are discovered to be too inadequate, especially when we are in desperate situations. In Summer, we want to test out the tools we had gained in Spring. We cannot wait to be in the middle of the ocean to determine if we really know how to swim. We cannot hang from the edge of a cliff to decide what tools we should have brought to climb.

Coming into Summer with the immature outlook of Spring can bring its own consequences, especially when we are tenacious about it.

While it is obvious that seasons gravitate in a one-way direction from one to another, the tools and amenities are unique to each season and the journey related to it. However, we may be able to use the tools of one season to speculate on our needs to devise and design tools for the other. In this way, history can be a worthwhile companion in helping us to understand the present and make predictions for the future. It is important that we do not encase ourselves into the molds of the past just because it may give us clues for the present or future.

The privileges and prerogatives of Spring are for us to enjoy fully for that season. When we graduate to summer, we make ourselves available for the amenities and responsibilities of summer. We do have to be careful, however, that we do not bring across the border any unresolved issues and stereotype attitudes to implement into our Summer adventures. If we travel into Summer while still being prisoners of Spring, our systems will overheat very early in our journeys, and we will blame it on the system and assume that pouring more water, excuses and explanations will bring about a feasible balance.

You cannot bring about a balance with an imbalance, and once we are stuck in denial, we will continue to bounce around frantically in the prison of our limitations while journeying into the new era of challenges and responsibilities. It is absolutely crucial that we focus on the development of the traffic and keep steady on our path.

If our minds are preoccupied with unresolved issues of the past, we can easily be distracted from the circumstances of the present. If we have not fully conquered our spring, we risk losing the benefits, the enjoyments and the valuable lessons in our Summer.

If we travel into Summer while still being prisoners of Spring, our systems will overheat very early in our journeys

When we make our journey, we become a spectacle for others as we pass.

THE JOURNEY

If we were as alert as we should have been, we would have realized that one season graduates into another in this one-way direction towards fulfillment and perfection. What goes on in Spring is very relevant in certain ways to what will go on in Summer, since we are graduating to the next level of competence and consciousness in making the journey. To graduate, we must go through the process of qualifying and the ritual of being promoted. When you are confident from where you have come, and what it took to get to where you are now, then you have a good reason to go where you are going.

By the time we are done with Spring we should know what we want to do with our Summer. It was in Spring that we first shaped our aspirations, when the farms and swamps of our minds began to show the first signs of life. Tubers for the lily sent shoots up to the sky to welcome the sun and the rain. The dreams of fertile minds had spread like flowers of the field. Those dreams attracted every form of life; they migrated across the fields and the universe in search of greener pastures and nesting places under the same bright sun. They never complained about the hazards of their travel, or the uncertainties of their growth or existence. They simply ran their course single-mindedly, and paid their dues from what they earned, before they faded away. We saw them pass in full array to an unknown destination.

In like manner, when we make our journey, we become a spectacle for others as we pass.

Just as we look at birds, trees, and settings for purposes that are meaningful to us, there are others that may look to us similarly, for sustenance to their lives and their missions in the journeys that they make.

Everyone watches for a shining example, a symbol he or she can adopt or follow that will make life easier and more worthwhile. We can hardly resist this temptation because of the natural curious nature to look beyond ourselves for inspiration and guidance. This is what we did on the wet road of Spring, when the rain was unusually heavy or the wind seemed to want to blow us off of our path.

We go to school, to learn how to manage our steering better, and how to monitor our systems and our needs. We look up to our elders, our parents and our community leaders for a dose of the collective pool of knowledge and wisdom, until the time comes for us to adopt them as our own at our exit at the rest stop.

Summer provides its own freedom and possibilities if we are alert enough to recognize them.

The wet of Spring should have given us enough moisture to welcome the dryness of Summer. As students and minors, we had enjoyed the protection and guidance necessary for our growth, and there is no reason why we cannot continue in the same way on our own, especially since the lanes of life are all marked similarly. The fountain of youth in spring, however, may not always leave us enough moisture to survive the challenge of the desert conditions of Summer.

How many of us will be able to develop camel-like qualities to give the weary and the thirsty a ride to the oasis? Some of the inconsistencies of life may bring us flat tires when assurances are broken, and the people in whom we place our confidences may severely let us down. Quick fixes are an option, but when the weather is at its hottest, it is dangerous to rush to the water fountain, especially when the water is too dramatically cold. Each season brings its own challenges, and the more acclimatized we are to the inferences of our journey, the better we will enjoy it. We are likely to rob ourselves of this benefit or pleasure if we settle for any compromises that divert from the true test of our character and integrity. Even the process through which we make those compromises may lack some integrity of its own. To try to execute a compromise through another person is even worse, since by doing so, you put yourself at a crossroads of two different minds in two different worlds that are affected by two different sets of circumstances.

COMPROMISES

Life can become a very enriching and fulfilling journey if we are able to take every experience within the context for what it is worth, like a jewel waiting to be polished and fitted for the adornment of our lives. If we can only learn to view each precious moment as the first and last of its kind, from and through which we should make ourselves accountable, then there would be no need to settle for grand illusions of prospects we can only imagine and not fulfill. When we know we have dreams we cannot fulfill, we settle for dreaming just for the sake of it, and eventually have to deal with all kinds of compromises.

A compromise is a 'better-than-nothing' attitude that can permeate our lives like a disease, breaking down every healthy cell of our being if it becomes dominant in our thinking. While there are compromises that do not seem to rob us of our integrity, we still have to be mindful of what we may be sacrificing to fulfill them. We may empathize with someone who is in a hopelessly destitute situation and is willing to settle for a temporary fix. We may be willing and eager to help but lack the necessary resources. What we need to recognize is that, depending on the nature of the problem, a temporary fix may leave someone with a lasting scar or internal incision that may bleed for a lifetime to come.

The extent to which we feel the need to yield to entrapments in the course of our lives is the very extent to which our dreams can become too grand and lofty in their illusions, leaving us to become addictive to them. When our inner resolve is hampered or overwhelmed by our habit of compromising, we can develop inferiority complexes for everything to the extent where these complexes can become chronic habits. Dreams built around complexes and guilt can easily be transformed to serve the purpose of responding to the priority of dealing with our handicaps.

Dreams can be compulsions going out of control. The creative and emotional energies that could otherwise be channeled into fulfilling a worthwhile purpose in life can be misdirected to enhance or cover up on peripheral issues. This is how we get so engrossed in dealing with symptoms that we habitually circumvent the causes to why we get so entrapped in situations that force us to consider compromises or quick fixes.

Quick fixes avoid the bigger context that is crucial to finding solutions to any problem. They encourage us to stay off target, to mask our discomfort under all kinds of disguises or pretentious behavior in order to make the appearance that all is well, happy and prosperous with us. The danger is that all these perambulations can become established as a way of life, as a sort of legitimate culture with formulated rules and rituals that can evoke dreams and aspirations of their own. They can root themselves like cancer cells in legitimate society, pervading every level, high and low, sucking everything that is good and beneficial from our higher aspirations to serve its insidious purposes, until our social system, down to its constitution, is sucked dry to a state of anemia.

This culture creates its own demons out of well-intentioned citizens when it creates parallel economies that have attractive but short term benefits parasitically rooted into the legal and economic system of society. Like the *H. Pylori* bacteria, this culture can take the best out of the system in order to fatten its demons, and then deposits its waste for the rest of society to clean up. Its byproducts are the systems of malpractice within the legitimate professions in health, education, housing, and social work. It fosters the machinery of crime, corruption and exploitation that become capable of building dreams and empires of their own, even out of the ashes and debris from the destruction it has caused.

Out of this atmosphere of hopelessness come our youths to the feeding troughs, or on conveyor belts in gangs and valediction ceremonies, to feed on these grand illusions because it is the only hope that they know.

THE LANES OF TRAFFIC

As we hold to our path, we discover more of the realities of our world and ourselves, and then we come to realize that we can have a different view if we change our path. Every path has a paradigm or perspective of its own, with sites and markers geared to shaping opinions and consciousness that are compatible with that path. We can freely view life from the perspective of history, economics, religion, culture, or simply from an egocentric point of view we may have inherited from our early days of Spring. We may have learned that while driving on one highway lane, that we need to be aware and alert to other lanes and their users.

Switching lanes impulsively or erratically is a recipe for disaster; so we must develop a code of ethics for changing lanes. The ramifications for changing lanes have their own sophistication. First, we learn to do so gracefully so that our systems adequately adjust to help us focus on our new line of thinking.

Switching lanes impulsively or erratically is a recipe for disaster

We may not have the opportunity to explore or experience all the lanes of life before we cross the borders out of Summer. Now that we have come this far, it becomes necessary to try to experience every lane possible to get a different perspective through the eyes, thoughts and lives of others. To truly benefit from an unfamiliar lane, we must be mindful not to get too close to the driver ahead of us, so that we are able to maintain our self-composure and independence and not run the risk of rear ending them. Someone else's confidence and wisdom should not be adopted as our own, since these are qualities in life we can hardly borrow. We can merely emulate the good qualities we observe in the people we admire, but transforming these sentiments into action would require staying in that lane for a while and getting our focus adjusted to the demands of that world.

Those we call heroes are the conquerors of circumstances through following the dictates of their own minds, for they are usually too preoccupied in working out their own solutions to even bother copying someone else. We may be inspired by the techniques of proponents and master practitioners, but until such a time when we can assimilate to the challenges we undertake and apply our own personal touches to it, we will be travelers in life who allow ourselves to be guided by other people's brake-lights. We may do better in our own deliberations by refining or redefining our feedback from the lessons we have learned, and readjusting our core values and strategies accordingly, instead of adulating other people's accomplishments, even when they are plated over in silver and gold.

THE SUMMER REST STOP

What is peculiar about the seasons is how in as many ways that they are similar, they are very different. In each season, we look at the same sky, trees, traffic and highway lanes, and even rest stops, and realize that they always change in one way or another. Even though they structurally remain the same, other factors change around them

The Summer rest stop is the time and place to take the opportunity to evaluate and assess

in relation to their position or functions, which influences the way we look at or respond to them. This is particularly so at the rest stop.

As you mature, your attitude to everything changes accordingly. You know why you want to stop, what to look for, and how to make the rest stop work to your utmost benefit. This is the time and place to take the opportunity to evaluate and assess what we have learned about ourselves, the world, and the process of the journey of life itself. Here, certain aspects and issues we develop on our journey may advance to a momentum of crisis proportions, and we can become very self-conscious of the way we choose to entertain ourselves or have fun. Our philosophy of fun may vary according to our level of sophistication, or what path we have been traveling through on our way. Fun can be as egocentric, sadistic, or wholesome as we want it to be. We can give ourselves a treat or we can still be of service to others while having fun.

The manner in which we procure our enjoyment is a clear indication of our philosophy of life itself, and the paths we are likely to choose in our travels. There are several levels of enjoyment in life, like anything else, that are available to us at any given time from which we can choose to saturate our senses. There is the lowest standard of instant gratification of the senses, which is the fulfillment of a need, physical, emotional, social or political, that we all get engaged or even entrapped in at some time or other. It would do us some good to fulfill these needs, for they are temporary, mundane and very routine.

We must feed our bodies, rest and exercise on a regular basis, so why not try to engineer some fun in performing these daily routines? While it is necessary, and even compulsory, to relieve our bodies of combustions, the attitude with which we execute these functions determine their benefits and success. Combustion involves the processing of extracting unwanted substances, even to its final stages. Our minds have a different story to tell when it engages in this process.

If only we can recognize the benefits of the ordinary, or even repugnant experiences in our daily interaction with our fellow human beings, we can enrich our souls routinely with the jewels that we extract. We may then see that the end products are worthy of a compost of wisdom to be recycled indefinitely for the benefit of mankind.

It is, however, a paradox in and of our human nature to discard our jewels on the wayside and focus on the pot of gold that is over the hill beyond the rainbow. We tend to categorize our experiences to determine their hierarchy according to the categories we have adopted or were given from our upbringing. In looking beyond the present, we fail to extract the benefits of our local resources in anticipation of grand illusions that exist beyond our means or capacities.

With every opportunity we miss to empower ourselves with this local source of genuine wisdom, we set limitations upon ourselves that become little prisons in our minds. We get obsessed with movie stars, successful athletes, and comic book heroes, and dis-acknowledge ourselves as the superstars of our own world, polishing the chains on our own hands and legs and the padlocks on our minds.

ASPIRATIONS

While it can be beneficial to look over and beyond ourselves to boost our aspirations, this is only possible when we can do so in relation to the present, and looking within ourselves to take the first steps towards the fulfillment of that goal. There are aspirations that are empty, merely adopted to make someone look good to others and to give the impression that the person parading with them is ambitious or intelligent. On the other hand, there are aspirations that start with little steps that can expand upon a pyramid of ideas that further expand to endless possibilities of all we can do or be. Those are the kinds of aspirations that attend to simple details, to the needs of people and the wider society, to the here and now and the little things we do in the ordinary events of life.

Aspirations can be the ladder on which we climb to the next level of endeavors in our pursuit towards perfection and heavenly bliss.

Life presents us with the challenges that take us to the next level of our consciousness, even when we tend not to recognize these as such. Therein lies the elements of fun embedded within these challenges, and the satisfaction of overcoming them one phase at a time. Even the greatest challenges of life can be fun and bring us happiness in advance once we know that the end result will be wisdom and enlightenment. All these aspirations can combine to create a lifestyle which concurrently brings pleasure at every endeavor. Life, with all its pains, inconsistencies and downturns, can be fun if we are able to adjust our focus on the way we look at it and the manner in which we live it.

RESPONSIBILITIES

In the Summer season of our lives, we should be acquainted enough with the routines to realize that all travel involves making decisions and taking action on them. Driving involves steering, accelerating, and making decisions about our destinations. We give ourselves the license to drive in this life when we accept the responsibilities for our actions in fulfilling our aspirations.

We all have capabilities, talents, and dreams. We also have physical bodies with wonderful and appropriate body parts and systems wonderfully connected to synchronize with each other. It is our responsibility to find out what our gifts or advantages are, how to use them and further enhance them. Some of us may come to realize that by the time we finally get competent enough to travel in full rhythm within a season, it seems to be already over, and we find ourselves embarking on a new season that imposes new rules and demands.

The common denominator in the journey is change. History may seem to repeat itself, but those who have made history are those who have changed the course of it. The patterns are the clues or indications, not the molds in which we fit ourselves. Each one of us is as unique as our fingerprints, our personality and our destiny, and we have a responsibility to craft our own history in our contribution to history itself. Being unique in your contribution does not imply that you should make changes purely to stroke your own ego. History is made through change that seeks improvement, not by sticking around a person or an issue like a stagnant pool with carcasses within.

When we focus on our egocentric pursuits in the travels of this life, we become like carcasses that bloat in the cesspool, holding hostage a whole thirsty generation that is waiting to get a healthy drink so they can move on to more wholesome ways of life. There is nothing more unfortunate than to see things that are intended for good being used to serve corrupt purposes. That is what we do when we utilize that which is wise when we conduct business that is foolish. We have to be careful that we are not misinterpreting a good principle by unconsciously working against it.

It is good for us to dwell on the self, on the improvement of the spirit, body, and mind; but when we get obsessed with it to the point where we want to alter all circumstances around it to facilitate its dominance, what we have left is a conceited, useless, and obnoxious obstruction in history. We will be worth nothing to history unless our contributions help history to flow, to sterilize the cesspool, to create flowing brooks and rivers in the desert for mankind to drink from to refresh and renew on the journey to perfection.

We make history when we move the rock that frees the river, and when we ignite revolutions that help society to grow.

A passenger may be a long term hitchhiker

A PARTNER OR PASSENGER

There comes a time in the course of our travels, especially during the heat of Summer, when we feel the desire for a companion to share our challenges, aspirations and the fun of our life's journey. This connection is better made while we are indulging ourselves at our rest stop, where our spirits are temporarily released from the obligations of direct traffic. Here we can focus on our needs, not only for leisure and relaxation, but also for the continuation of our journey. A passenger may be a long term hitchhiker to whom we can find ourselves wholly or partly responsible,

71

and whose primary objective is to use the comforts we provide to facilitate their own journey at our expense.

Passengers have destinations of their own and may or may not be willing to pay their way. Someone who is willing to compensate has indirectly offered to buy your services, once you have agreed to their offer or request. There are subtle ways in which our standards and the integrity of our interaction with other people can be altered if we are not careful with the agreements we make, or the nature of the interactions we accommodate. If we feel desperate or insecure enough to settle hastily with our choice of a passenger, then we should consider the implications of that relationship, including its responsibilities.

Someone who hitchhikes on your journey with selfish intentions but under the pretense of being a friend will be preoccupied with finding ways to benefit the relationship.

A passenger's responsibility involves that of verbal support and trust while he or she enjoys our assurance of safety and that he or she will be dropped off at the desired destination, not ours. The comforts we either provide directly or facilitate are clearly invested in their present and future aspirations, if we continue to make them available.

Our passenger's strategy in life may be built on using temporary supports along the way to cater towards grand illusions, and our sincere and congenial spirit will provide the cushions for such a luxurious ride. His or her priority may very well be to assess how long these comforts will be available, so that he or she can plan ahead to make the necessary transition to the next phase of the journey.

Although passengers are temporary companions, they can create a void when they leave, if the facilities of your goodwill have been the ladder or bridge they had used to fill the void in theirs. They can get easily agitated if you suffer a breakdown or a flat tire, and in many cases will promptly abandon you to hitchhike for another ride. Passengers who are preoccupied with the urgency of their own affairs become more of a distraction or nuisance because they lack the sensitivity to recognize, much less acknowledge, the disruption of traffic or the possible accident they may have caused.

When the need for a copilot overwhelms us, it is obviously more advantageous to acquaint ourselves with someone who has partner potential. In business, as in life, the best partners have common goals that inevitably complement each other, enabling them to better meet the challenges in each other's lives. They recognize the importance of copiloting to aid in doing whatever is necessary to close the loopholes of what would otherwise be an imperfect life. The consequences for the decisions they make and the actions they take are viewed in the same light by partners, since the level of empathy is high for each other's dreams and aspirations. When partners socialize, it enables them to search for clarifications that will gauge the fit for a wholesome union.

Genuine friendship and trust results in a level of bonding that can and often does develop into a passion. An attachment of this nature certainly changes the nature of the journey, although hopefully not the focus.

When two travelers become partners, the first thing they will do is make room for each other, not in two vehicles but in one. There is the necessary ritual of processing the qualities and luggage of one vehicle to the next, and determining what they will continue their journey with and what they will definitely leave behind. For some partners, this ritual can be very painful and may take longer than it should. The other partner should understand it is his or her duty to wait until the last relics of that ritual are in place and that the past has truly become a memory to be left behind forever.

They both know that to nurture attachments to those relics left behind would be detrimental to the journey and to the partnership that they have made; so in an act of spiritual cremation, they place their disposable relics on the pyre and set it alight in their hearts together. What they should have left is only the necessities to lighten their journey, as they need room for the strength and confidence it will take to endure a long journey and also the capacity to have fun along the way. The added security of each other makes the journey more worthwhile, with sights to see, treats to share and each other's voices like music to the ear. When they leave this rest stop, they leave behind the greatest fear one can ever take on a journey: the fear of being alone.

Being alone is a paradox all by itself. It can enrich and it can paralyze; it helps to strengthen us, but it can enslave us with the need for company; it can be a blessing to help us find ourselves, or curse us with the feeling that we are the center of the universe. It is all the more a paradox because even as we enjoy a fruitful relationship with our partner, we can never really escape the responsibilities we have to ourselves and the need to retreat into the sanctuary of our minds for strength and reformation.

It is this necessary process of self-rejuvenation that partners can mistakenly view with suspicion as a signal to the end of their solid union. The purpose of a union is to strengthen and not to weaken, for each partner has brought to the union a set of unique skills and abilities that are peculiar for each other. Those qualities need to be enriched and sharpened along the way to strengthen the bond that first brought them together.

The purpose of a union is to strengthen and not to weaken

A partner may try, but can do very little to enhance the inherent qualities the other possesses. He or she simply needs to facilitate the process of the other, undertaking that responsibility to himself or herself with the understanding that it brings added power and cohesion to the partnership. Like two cells needing liquid and electricity to bond, partners need to bring with them the force and renewed conviction to make them less vulnerable to free radicals in the challenges of life. That involves occasionally making room for each other to employ unique skills, even if it involves exercising a franchise within the relationship. We must be careful of not holding our partner to higher level of expectations and performance than we ourselves are able to keep. We may end up using valuable effort and energy to condemn and criticize instead of helping to support and forgive.

It is important to step aside when the need arises for a partner to exhort authority in his or her area of specialty with the support of the other, without reservation. In order to fulfill this responsibility effectively, each partner needs those opportunities to strengthen and grow within to maintain the status and the competence to continue the partnership. It is the accumulated strength and contribution of both partners that determines the status of the partnership.

The responsibilities and obligations a partner has to himself or herself are just as important and equivalent to those he or she has to the partnership and to the other partner. When we plunge headfirst into a partnership only to immerse ourselves in the passions and sentiments of being together, we risk turning true virtues into vices that create contrasts that set both partners on a road to competition and final confrontation. To abandon ourselves in the process of enjoying our partner's virtues is equivalent to depriving your partner of one half of the fulfillment of those virtues.

We need to retain our unique qualities, if we are confident that we know what they are, and then polish and enrich them with every opportunity we get to do so. In order for those qualities to serve us best, we need not only to preserve them but also protect them from any contamination or associations with loose ethical or moral behavior. How we behave reflects what we will eventually become, even if it is not our original intention. It is safer to try not to play games with our integrity, as it is our most valuable resource. If there is one basis on which our partner bases his or her trust in us, it is their reliance on our integrity. That includes the assurance that by our very nature, we will hardly condescend to a lower standard of behavior and ethics than what he or she had associated with us from the beginning.

Personal integrity can be protected and maintained by no one else but the person concerned. No one can protect us from something that we deliberately invite unto ourselves. Even being associated with persons of low character can arouse suspicion and fear about the basis of that connection, which can make our partner very uneasy and uncomfortable. It is not necessary to put your partner's loyalty to the test in ways that question your integrity. The challenges of life will do enough of that along the way.

You do not have to stage any kind of scenario to prove yourself to your partner as this tends to create splinters and residue that can lay around or return to haunt you both. You and your inherent qualities are valuable assets to your partner, who relies heavily on the assurance that those qualities were not illusions or staged performances. To bring a partner to the point of questioning your integrity or your sincerity would be equivalent to striking a thunderbolt to the very foundation of your partnership.

RESPONSIBILITIES TO THE SELF

Our integrity not only defines us as persons or virtues that we possess, but it also determines the duties and obligations to which we are bound. We can stand tall like a tower of virtue, but it is how we stand up to the storms of life that reveals our true character. It is our duty to keep refining and redefining our innate qualities through deliberate efforts at self-improvement.

Even monuments of stone and bronze need to be cleaned and restored to their original beauty before they can even appear worthy of their value and status.

Would not the fragile and unpredictable nature of us humans need that same process of inner cleansing to reexamine our intentions, our philosophy and aspirations? We need to find moments or create opportunities to be at rest within ourselves, so that the process of inner cleansing can begin to clear our vision and reflect the inner light that exists within us. That is the light our partner needs in order to connect with us during the ongoing challenges of the travels of life.

Every person's approach to self-refinement or self-improvement can be a source of encouragement and inspiration to their partner. It is our duty to provide that stimulation from within the partnership to serve as an incentive to each other. When our minds get stagnant with overworked ideas and principles, we fall asleep spiritually and can fall victim to all kinds of contaminations. We seek out and attend workshops or seminars where similar minds assemble for a common purpose, read books, or find other ways to connect to a higher source of power and inspiration.

Some of us pray or meditate if we know how, but all are different paths of self-improvement that belong to or emerge from the same route. As we incorporate these processes of upliftment and enrichment as normal into our lifestyles, we will need to also remember the world outside us and get ourselves back on track. We need to step back from our inner sanctuary to rejoin our partner on the journey or change places in the driving seat. The good thing is that we've had our nap, and are refreshed and ready to move on.

Our responsibility to ourselves is a gracious complement of our responsibility to our partner. As an extension of us in this union, our partners need the same prerogatives, privileges, and facilities to grow and expand to the fullest of their potential. They are not standbys, substitutes, or prestigious servants in waiting. They have dreams and aspirations that now include us and our dreams, which compound their responsibilities even more.

We need to make room for our partners to grow into their world and take advantage of all the possibilities that are open to them.

These possibilities can hardly be dominated by assumption or speculation if we help to make the bed comfortable and guard our partners in their sleep. It may involve rearranging the space so that both of you can fit. When we retreat into our inner sanctuary to enrich and redirect our talents and skills, we understand the need to do so for our own health and well-being.

QUALITIES OF A GOOD WORKING PARTNER

It is, therefore, relative to reflect on what our partner's needs are and engineer a retreat for him or her as well. The satisfactions and benefits we enjoy from our perspective can now be reflected into our partner's world with our tenacious supervision. Your partner will be forever grateful if you show that you realize, or better still, verbally acknowledge how important he or she has become in your life. Your gratitude and praise need not be confined to words and token gifts but rather expanded into a way of life that increases the fun in everything you do together. Your obligations to each other could be the basis on which you extract the fun out of the things you do in life together.

To even begin to qualify to be a partner or to get one for yourself, you need first to get over your obsession with yourself and become obsessed instead with those things that would make your partner happy and satisfied being a partner with you. That is not being simply intellectual or academic by knowing what they are, but rather inculcating those qualities into your character and daily life to eventually become a part of who you are. Your partner will be attracted to those qualities and associate them with you.

Knowing those qualities is crucial, but agreeing on them is the purpose of your negotiations during courtship. To begin a relationship before the negotiations are complete would be tragic and hazardous for living. Both you and your potential partner have the serious responsibility to prepare for each other, before you even undertake the responsibility of being together. That is why the negotiations are very necessary before you consummate the relationship. Agreements may need to be reached that areas in which each is lacking or unprepared, each will help the other, even if the whole relationship functions temporarily as a work in progress. A relationship that has been prematurely or haphazardly consummated when parts for the togetherness do not fit, will never be truly connected. It is better to stand by than to keep struggling to stand on each other.

These obligations form the basis on which the partnership becomes an institution with its own needs and demands. The partnership becomes a sanctuary that is our assurance that there is a copilot by our side, and also is our insurance that caters to most of our shortcomings that we have yet to realize. It is from within the sanctuary of our partnership that we exercise our new confidence to go forward on our journey and confront the challenges of this life. That sanctuary needs to be maintained and protected and given the level of reverence and respect like a prized monument within our hearts and minds. The foundation of this sanctuary is based on the sincerity of our intentions and the integrity of our character. Like a secret society with sworn contracts and rituals, a true partnership exerts a tenacious will on its partners to submit to a code of ethics, so that the partnership can take on a life of its own.

Our obligations to ourselves and our partner become separate and distinct, yet inseparably connected with our obligation to the partnership itself. A relationship is based on an unwritten or unspoken oath that both partners have taken in their minds that sets the tone for the nature of the interaction that follows. It establishes that common ground or rationale whereby both partners adapt to accommodate each other and make themselves worthy of the intrigues and pleasures associated with the partnership. Keeping pace with each other and the outside traffic is one such obligation to maintain good balance and equilibrium, but it is also one routine we follow to stay alert and get in line with each other. The partnership enables us to think and behave in peculiar ways to strengthen and enrich the partnership. As the partnership transforms and evolves to another level, the nature of our obligations change, and we are compelled to develop new skills and tools to maintain and protect the integrity of it.

Half-hearted participants can hardly tolerate a sanctuary, much less maintain or protect it. When we are at the level of maintaining the sanctuary of our partnership, we impulsively perform certain duties according to the needs that arise. We look ahead of the traffic to anticipate projected challenges while our partner takes care of any immediate concerns that are under the current circumstances.

Both partners develop a coordination and rhythm that becomes a routine within the partnership that requires no explanation or prequalification. They know it is incumbent on them to keep monitoring the rear view mirrors even as they go forward in their many ventures.

They are alert to the schedules and appointments on life's busy one-way street. Being forced to come off at an exit to pick up after ourselves is never good for a partnership. We could miss each other in the conflict of urgencies and end up outside the sanctuary and back on the highway alone. This is why we need to get into line on time to do what has to be done, so that the journey remains a journey of progress and not a series of apologetic quick stops to ferment over after unfinished business.

A partnership can hardly afford the deadweights of minds that are preoccupied with petty vendettas and fancies, while procrastinating on their duties towards the upkeep of their sanctuary. If ever a partnership has to indulge in a retreat, it should be a calculated one that is designed to prepare themselves to go forward. After you have parked for a while to review your options and check your maps, analyze the possibilities, for it is necessary to retreat from the parking lot and reacquaint yourself with the responsibilities of driving.

Partners never retreat just to go back to serving egotistical nostalgia that is outside the sanctuary of the partnership. Their egos and aspirations have become fused into one within the sanctuary of the partnership; and they think, speak, feel and even dream in unison.

**Being aware of our environment is necessary for our safety
and survival.**

ONTO THE HIGHWAY TOWARDS FALL

By the time we are ready to leave the rest stop to rejoin the highway of life, we are better informed, more equipped and skilled than when we first started in Spring. Experience may have tested our resolve but we are now more aware of our privileges and limitations. The paradox of our travels is that while all our knowledge and skills are acquisitions from the past, they do not necessarily prepare us for the future.

Obviously we can make adjustments and predictions, but basically the future cannot be measured or calculated. The level of our awareness dictates the level of our response to situations as they arise, and also guides our competence in making appropriate connections and applying the right skills with the right tools. We must recognize however, how sophisticated we have become as we mature into life, and the responsibilities we have entailed subsequently. Perhaps it is a good thing that we do not know what is on the journey ahead, or that lack of challenge may make the journey become so empty and meaningless that we may lose the impetus to even hold our steering.

Being physically aware of our environment can be very rudimentary, if not mundane sometimes, but it is nevertheless necessary for our safety and survival. It helps us to keep to our lane and prevents us from falling asleep at the wheel. However, our sophistication has made us more spiritually aware of our sense of purpose that makes every mile covered joyful and fulfilling. It is the spiritual that determines the level of the physical, for what we do can never be compared to what we are driven to do. While there are physical motivations that arise from needs of all kinds, they are nevertheless physical, and can be satisfied after a short diversion. It is the spiritual that enables us to help keep the physical in its proper place, so that we are not preoccupied with the relentless pursuit of hollow sensations that amount to addictions and lust.

We can hardly afford to sacrifice our higher intentions for our lower satisfactions. At this phase of our journey, we have got to make ourselves accountable for the responsibilities that are entrusted upon us.

The partnership and the extensions that come with it are all part of the journey. The partnership may have produced offspring that are extensions of both of us, and both partners will have to adjust to the concept that these offspring are there on the back seat as privileged passengers. Their privileges do not extend to the point where they are allowed to sit in the front seat, much less to dominate it.

Children come to go, not to stay.
They are a part of us, not the
whole.

Partners can become divided in their philosophy of parenthood after the children arrive, and can become distracted from the sanctuary of the partnership that sincerely welcomes the children to the journey. That division can cause either or both partners to abandon the sanctuary to give priority to their allegiance to their offspring.

An abandoned or neglected sanctuary can get very cold and uncomfortable long before the fall season comes along, which forces all parties concerned to seek better shelters elsewhere, even in the midst of travel. Who will drive or choose the lane when each party in the system wants to go a separate route, in a different lane? That is the kind of distraction that can cause serious accidents on the highways of life, making litter of precious lives and dreams strewn all over for the sympathy and education of other travelers and spectators.

REJOINING THE HIGHWAY TOWARD AUTUMN

As we rejoin the highway into the corridors of life, we can feel the sense of accomplishment and gratitude that we have come this far. In life, we graduate to the level of our needs. It is the spirit that takes us beyond the level of our needs to enable us to see beyond the windscreens into our minds. The more we know, the more we are able to do, but it is the spirit that empowers us to challenge ourselves with the realms beyond our capacity and imagination to explore that which we do not know.

The highways of life are adorned with opportunities galore if we only have the eyes to see them. They are like flowers reaching out as from an orchard to be fertilized. They are only ripe once for the taking; and once we pass them, they are never the same. We must travel with minds alert enough to anticipate and recognize their presence, with hands ready and equipped to reap the benefits, and with facilities ready to process and store towards posterity.

Spring had brought us flowers blessed with the rain; Summer brought us sunshine; and Fall will bring its own gifts only if and when our minds are tuned to welcome them with the relevant frame of mind. The gifts of nature, like the gifts of life, are ever present and ready for our perusal, and to shower us abundantly with its virtues. When we approach them with our predigested and often contaminated notions, we can misinterpret, misuse or abuse these virtues, robbing ourselves of their benefits.

There are those that are ours for the taking; like rain and sunshine, fruits of the earth, water and fields, for us to service and satisfy our physical needs. There are those that are better off staying where they are, to service or decorate the earth and to maintain the grandeur of the universe for every season, time and place. The rocks with their vines and fungi, the waterfalls that provide chapters for the streams to flow, the lilies of the field and insects and animals big and small, are no more or less important than the partner by our side or the offspring in our back seat.

When we impose ourselves upon nature and the universe, to discriminate against and categorize the gifts of nature to accommodate our egocentric view of life, we develop the warped vision and philosophy that can haunt us throughout our travels. Looking beyond the windshield is not enough for safe and worthwhile travel; it is being able to see and observe to be able to understand what is crucial to our survival on the road. It is possible for us to see backwards while we are traveling forward.

When we view all nature from the perspective of what we would like it to be, we imprison our minds within the tunnels of obsession, shutting off all the other qualities of what we actually see to focus only on what we want to see. That is equivalent to navigating our journey from behind a frosted windshield, expecting the rest of the world to yield to our desires and expectations. That only happens on treadmills where the path comes to us and we merely have to walk it. There is nothing more that robs us of the joys of this life than the conveyor belt mentality, where everything is fed to us cafeteria-style and our only responsibility is to serve ourselves in a feast from the generosity of the government or charitable agencies under what may be false or pretentious motives.

To live in an egocentric world of our own and expect the world to yield to our every whim and fancy is like expecting all the rules of traffic to change to accommodate our presence. What makes it more problematic is when we let this kind of philosophy infiltrate our partnership, forcing partners to adopt strategies that engineer successes at almost impossible odds.

An egocentric philosophy of life can drive us to the point of desperation to realize the fulfillment of our dreams. Our obsession with ourselves can blind us from realizing that our misguided goals will heavily depend on everyone and everything, including nature itself, abandoning their routines and responsibilities in order to service our wishes and expectations.

INTERNAL DISTRACTIONS

When we become so preoccupied with dealing with our handicaps, we can put ourselves at a very great disadvantage in spite of our level of sophistication in being able to come this far on our journey. Our sophistication implies that we have acquired some wisdom and foresight to make sensible decisions, but the trials and tests of the journey of life demand ability and action, not qualifications and awards. We assume that someone in a partnership with the responsibility of offspring in the backseat will have the sophistication to look and think beyond the dashboard and through the windshield.

How can we be in the full course of life's journey, in the midst of traffic, and still be fiddling with the gadgets on our dashboard to find out what lane we want to be in and what is our ultimate goal or destination? How can we be busy trying to find ourselves when we are already the integral part of something bigger? How can we drive and play our Xbox games, with our loved ones and our partner in the passenger seats? Some of us do not play games with our fingers and toys, but do it in our heads, focusing on the myths and enticements, the prejudices and the beliefs.

There are things that get in the way of your journey with your partner that have nothing to do with the journey itself. Even the vehicle we drive sometimes can become such an obsession to us, it becomes difficult for us to drive it as we should. We can so be preoccupied with our love for our vehicle that we may even forget to show love to our loved ones who are in it with us. Some of us are so preoccupied with loving things, we have lost the incentive to love people. Even the journey itself can become such an obsession, we forget our obligations of travel and begin spinning our tires at the same place instead. The aggrandizement of having grown up or reached a certain age is not reliable proof that we have lived life as we should. Many of us just simply exist from day to day and year to year, and never really traveled the journey of life. We lived our lives on a platform or stage, which we moved with us along the way to prevent ourselves from touching the road.

Some of us get too obsessed with ourselves and our ego to even see clearly where we are going. Therefore, we need our things and our toys to keep us occupied and satisfied with ourselves. That is why we hardly see beyond the windscreen of the circumstances in which we travel and are always taken by surprise at every turn. It is quite hazardous to drive ourselves instead of the vehicle or even to get so obsessed with our love for the vehicle that we allow the vehicle to drive us. When we do not know our priorities in life, we should not drive until we learn what are those priorities.

Our lack of resolve and our hesitation may already have begun to affect traffic and the lives of others in or alongside our lane. Already, we have become a potential hazard to ourselves and others because we have chosen to see what we want to see instead of what we actually see ahead, around, and behind us. We are in a world that is moving, so when we are standing still we can potentially be the target for collisions that could be deadly not only to those closest to us, but to every other traveler who assumed we ought to be moving.

LEARNING TO LOOK AS WE TRAVEL

Travelers can hardly afford to accommodate the luxury of others' hesitations in the flow of traffic, much less a sudden complete stop. If we have not yet assimilated the mysterious workings of nature and the human mind, we can explore all these at the rest stop where we can get our minds in the proper perspective for our journey. There is always something beautiful about the mysteries of nature and how the human mind works. If we do not go through the ritual to enjoy that which is beautiful, we can hardly acquire the frame of mind to differentiate that which is ugly.

There are innumerable ways in which nature displays its beauty, not only visually, but also in its functions. Nature exhibits coordination, cooperation, self-sacrifice, and diligence which we humans are very quick to admire, even though nature does not require the acknowledgement. There is something aesthetic about the assurance of sunrise and sunset, and the exhibition of which are presented in all their glory. The sun does not complain about not having any sick days or vacation time. The flowers that we admire and the vegetation that varies the landscape all work with the ritual of coordination that we cannot grasp during the fleeting moment that we pass by, but we nevertheless enjoy them. There is something edifying about observing and studying them, their colors, their movement, and their form, if we would just take the time to do so.

The birds and the bees may seem insignificant

The birds and the bees may seem very insignificant to us humans, but compared to us, they have been where we can never go and have seen what we may never see. These insignificant looking organisms, with a lifespan that is too short to mention, have covered more miles against greater odds than we can ever imagine to fulfill their mission, and on schedule too. We may think that we are passing them, but they may actually be passing us, on their way to fulfill part of their mission before sundown. They work with the wind and the sun, the water and the earth, the butterflies and the trees in a rhythm of give and take, with a single-minded focus that benefits all. There is something beautiful about that machinery and how it works, if only we could not just observe it, but also adopt it into our lives. Nature can achieve this perfection because it does not discriminate against itself, categorize with low intentions like we display, or complain about its partners like the wind and the rain. It sings a song instead and enjoys the precious privilege of being there in existence.

BEAUTY AND UGLINESS

When we are able to appreciate the things that are beautiful in our journey in life, we are better able to differentiate and even appreciate the things that are ugly. Nothing is actually ugly in nature, especially in appearance or form.

---

*The concept of ugliness is a human
invention that conforms to our
egocentric, insular and single-
minded motives to categorize and
compare everything to our selfish,
narrow perspective.*

The ugliness I refer to here pertains to our actions and intentions in the manner that we deliberately manipulate the good to extract that which is bad. Everything was good about the sunshine in Summer, yet we complained that it was too hot. Then we crossed the border into Fall and complained that the wind was cold. The rain will not escape our ungrateful lips when we are having a bad day, when in fact it is performing its role in the cycle of nature to replenish the earth with moisture.

The tendency to be ungrateful is one of the expressions of ugliness that we offer in exchange for the reliability of nature on which our environment depends. While the sun faithfully rises from behind the horizon, we focus on the rain making the road slippery. Beauty and ugliness are not confined to appearances whereby the external characteristics become the final judgment of character and personality, or indicators of premeditated thoughts and motives.

Nature in all its presumed ugliness, in action and in form, performs some of the most generous and wholesome tasks. Even the deadliest storm in all its ferocity may, within the context of nature, be actually a buffet of niceties being poured onto the earth for its benefit. Observing things with an aesthetic frame of mind enables us to see beyond the external form to the internal; to feel even before we see, hear or touch, and to know even before we are taught.

The animals hold no grudges that interrupt their missions, which enables them to take full advantage of their short time to enjoy the gifts of nature in ways that are unique and specific for them. We humans claim to have the authority to determine who or what is beautiful, and the tools we employ disqualifies the vast majority of the creations of nature.

We are often too obsessed with the politics of ugliness to be able to determine what is beautiful. We tend to look beyond the object or person for what they are worth inherently to first determine what they are worth to us. When we choose to be the center and the end-product of everything, we are indulging in the politics of ugliness that eventually shape the world in which live. We can become addicted to alien desires and needs that can collectively entrap us into lifestyles that rely heavily on greed, hate, discrimination and lust.

---

*A person caught in these lifestyles is
more likely to lack human empathy
or discern beauty in other people,
other things or events.*

THE CULTURE OF UGLINESS

Ugliness can sometimes seem beautiful because of the temporary pleasure it provides, but it can open up an insatiable appetite to alter the operations of the rest of the world to feed into the frenzy that we have created around ourselves. Since nature itself would never partake in such abnormal operations, we humans can always form special groups and create subcultures of our own to accommodate our egocentric fantasies. These subcultures require special conditions that reflect the philosophies and priorities of those concerned, but with the exclusion of everything else. When we have succeeded in establishing that vacuum for ourselves, then we have no alternative but to project the power structure we have created to pervade every level of society to service our aspirations.

A cancer of one mind can become an epidemic in society, creating its own lane of traffic at the inconvenience of everybody else. An experiment or diversion into the politics of ugliness can develop into a full blown institution, establishing its own morals and ethics within the arteries and machinery of society.

When we involve ourselves in the culture of ugliness, our actions and our tendencies become the magnets that draw to us forces that have similar inclinations. We bring litter into the highways of life, things that clutter the main arteries of our once ambitious selves.

When we become greedy, we attract forces that deal and trade in greediness, although they call it business and insist that they have done nothing wrong. If we want to be selfish, there are forces that make a business out of taking advantage of the misfortunes and anxieties of others.

There are ugly currencies flowing within the business world, that change lanes and faces, that trade emotions and high ideals, and purchase loyalty and truth. If we want to deal with hate, we do not have to change lanes, since it seems interconnected to each, giving out rewards and incentives like confetti pouring from the sky from a victory parade. There is no limit to which hate will go to create a celebration of itself, even if it has to wear the mask of love to give itself the appearance of a sense of purpose.

THE PRODUCTS OF UGLINESS

From religion to academia to ethnicity and culture, hate seeks out every possible platform to put on a worthwhile show to justify its existence and mission. When the mind of man is intoxicated with sufficient doses of it, it can become convinced that hate's most hideous actions towards other fellow men are labors of love.

The true journey of a fulfilling life can become cluttered with slogans and allegiances of all kinds like stickers on our windshield, insomuch that we can hardly see past them to keep our mind on the traffic. Under the influence of hate, the lane in which we travel can get increasingly restricted to what is left for us to see. Hate and greed combined can seriously restrict the arteries of our thinking and, consequently, our vision to the extent that they can hijack our dreams and aspirations, refurbishing them for us to carry as banners of our own. Once we get intrigued with banners, we tend to want to collect more and more of them, for greed and hate are closely related to envy in a family of obsessions that vehemently support each other.

Envy sets the precedent for our interaction with other travelers based on what we think they should or should not have in relation to what we have. We cater to address our emotions according to the level, quality and quantity of that person's credentials, so that we can see a millionaire as mundane when put next to a billionaire.

Our literature, our entertainment, and our entire state of mind become alienated from nature and instead focused on lottery windfalls, wealth, luxury clothing, cars and mansions that will always probably exist beyond our capacity or means. Our obsessions dig us deeper and deeper into a pit of inferiority complexes as we struggle to find a place for ourselves at the periphery of the environment we have adopted.

UGLY POLITICS OF SURVIVAL

Having drifted so far away from ourselves and the real world, we resort to relying heavily on community leaders, politicians, and heroes to manage what is left for us. Suddenly, we lack the desire or competence to take care of ourselves and rely desperately on the advocacy of politicians and celebrities to represent us.

The inferiority and superiority complexes on which we have built our world can begin to control us and make demands of us to create some sort of balance from the many inconsistencies that prevail around us. Now we exist outside and beyond ourselves, relying on the opinions, decisions, and actions of the other people we have convinced ourselves were more important than we are.

Meanwhile, along life's highway and always approaching unfamiliar territory, we still have to maneuver ourselves around the many hazards and distractions that constantly require our utmost attention. First, there is that unexpected bump that startles us when the smooth familiar surface of our lane runs out. The sudden turbulence can jerk the steering from our grasp, if we are not careful. It may not be as simple as a piece of litter left behind by a careless or unaware driver, or a carcass not promptly dragged away. It may be a slow leak, or a total blowout in the middle of traffic from a sharp implement left in our lane.

A financial emergency can strike our financial comfort like an upturned nail or a stray bullet, creating a temporary rupture in our lives and deep emotional void in our hearts because of its impact on our loved ones. There is always the very unexpected that comes upon us with our eyes wide open and our minds alert, that strikes us like black ice on a cold and windy day. There can be an incidental death or illness in the family, or an emotional clash of personalities with a furious exchange of words. These are all a part of the travel in which we have to learn to forgive ourselves and others for overreacting.

ELEMENTS OF DISTRACTION

There is more to the politics of travel than to worry about a few bumps on the road. These are some of the diversions in travel that add to the excitement and enrichment of life. What we need to be cautious about during travel are the distractions that are deliberately placed to grab our attention. These are usually deliberately placed to engage us for a reason.

Billboards shout their advertisements and advocates scream their messages on appropriate occasions. They both place themselves into strategic locations or situations so that they can get the best of our attention, in an opportune way that will burrow their concept or message like a seed into our subconscious to be nurtured by us through situations in our lives. The concept or message begins to imbed itself and spring roots after we allow them in, and then we find ourselves entrapped or addicted to whatever novel desire that was created to be fulfilled. A force that can make us want what we did not want originally is very precarious indeed.

How many of these entrapments
can we survive in a lifetime?

Some are so consuming they can make us put our entire life's earnings on ransom, and then find ourselves reduced financially to mere messengers that are only useful to carry out other people's errands. The people who are behind this power broking process call it advertising, and conclude that it is just a part of business, but they dedicate themselves to it with the tenacity of a predator.

They set goals and make predictions of how many customers will be ensnared, then target those who are not with more pervasive and aggressive tactics. Theirs is not a mission but a crusade to fulfill the proclamation of greed to guarantee that they can garnish the income and resources of every section of the population. Their crusade is viewed in the light of the philosophy of opposite. For convenience, we shall call this crusade the War of Opposites; since the victims seem to be happy and content, people assume that their aspirations are being fulfilled. Even governments call the practice of greediness a clear indication of prosperity and collectively countries call it trade.

The War of Opposites

Jerry S. Barry

THE WAR OF OPPOSITES

The War of Opposites is a full blown attack on nature and everything that is natural. It starts with the excessive exploitation of the earth's resources and its living things. It continues with us persuading ourselves that all the resources of the universe exist for our exclusive benefit and that we human beings are not accountable for our actions and how we use the resources of the earth. Again, the egocentric perspective empowers us to think that all other things exist for our benefit, and that we have the unlimited prerogative to use them as we choose.

There are trees to be garnished out of the forest to make paper, and there is oil to be sucked up from below. Fish have to be scooped up to suit our appetite and animals have to be slaughtered to fulfill our menus, or hunted as fair game for us to play. Our advantage of knowledge and technology seems bent in one direction only and that is to control and alter the workings of nature to satisfy only our needs, at the expense of all the elements that contribute to it.

The War of Opposites begins with this betrayal where we contribute to our self-destruction by exploiting or even eliminating to extinction the very sources that exist for our benefit. This pattern of self-destruction goes on at many levels. First, we overconsume and overharvest to the point where the ecosystem becomes exhausted or completely annihilated.

When we are starving and deprived, we try to reverse the famine by starting farms and nurseries on a mega scale to find a way to continue to exploit nature's resources. We are interested in nature only to the extent where it can feed, comfort, and entertain us and our offspring. Except for the selected few we reserve for our zoos and laboratories, we can afford to exterminate any animals and plants that do not serve us and leave the others to their own destruction.

Our confidence in the little we have learned from nature has bloated our egos to magnum proportions, so that we begin to see ourselves as masters of the universe because of the temporary advantages we enjoy. We impose our developmental ambitions to interrupt the chain of ecosystems that existed for centuries, so that we can execute our version of beauty and balance in the world. The emphasis now for us is no longer coexistence in nature but self-preservation and isolation.

We design our houses to be self-contained, with central air and solar energy and temperature controlled interiors that isolate us from nature and from each other. We tend to be affected by this bipolar logic that we can exist in nature, alter and bend its resources to satisfy our needs and comforts, and then dismiss it altogether.

We now process our processed foods with colorful chemical nutrients in factories that can package it in the most convenient and attractive form suitable for advertising. We no longer eat but ingest to save ourselves the trouble of having to do things naturally and normally, so that we are gradually programmed to rely less on our natural functions and affect these through chemical interferences. We relentlessly usurp our bodies' natural qualities to inoculate them to function by proxy, without having to do what we normally have to do to keep ourselves healthy.

Our appetite for being egocentric has reached the climax where we are trying to alter ourselves out of existence.

EXTENDED EGOTISM

When our egotism reaches a certain proportion and is able to have its own way, our appetite for greediness and selfishness can open like the gorge of a bottomless pit. The egocentrism that feeds into the culture of ugliness will not be content with just having its own way with us and with nature. It must have more and more to function. Therefore, we have no choice but to turn on others like ourselves or on whoever else is available for consumption.

Our egotism had served us well in our Spring and even part of our Summer, but like a flower that has reached its prime, it was supposed to have been fertilized to give way to the birth of a good fruit. It was good to establish our self-esteem, our individualism and skills for self-survival. However, this sweet beautiful flower in the bloom of youth, when nurtured beyond its prime, can become a cancerous wart that can devour our personalities. It can camouflage and transform itself to conceal its true identity and purpose, finding ways through action and intent to portray itself to the very opposite of what it really is. We see it evident in those pampered youths who have never been made aware of responsibilities and limitations, and who use the loyalty of their parents and best friends as a vehicle to forward their ludicrous agenda. When we do not graduate to the level of our maturity, we will do what is necessary to compensate.

Everyone needs to visit the rest stop where he or she can get a tune up and seasonal balance. When we do not, we can potentially become a casualty of the highway, along with the other people with whom we associate.

The greatest tragedy that can
befall anyone is being involved in
a war that has nothing to do with
him or her.

Displaced personalities with out-of-tune egos can get coerced into any campaign or crusade that can be explained or expressed through their inferiority complexes. What would normally be a distraction for others can become an obsession with them. Criminal gangs and secret societies target such recruits to become their loyal foot soldiers to perform scavenger duties. If one such inconsistency can be of such detriment to society, what about the huge number of people amassing on the highways of life that get lured into the lane of hate as a result of poor education and bad parenting?

We get a graphic demonstration of this in the lifestyles of child prodigies and movie stars who have attained the wealth and power to indulge in their fantasies. Those of us who are smitten with the bug but do not have the power or the means, remain as silent but secret recruits, idolizing those very malcontents as our role models and indulging ourselves in any way we can. We keep hoping for a windfall that could make us millionaires for even one day so that we can live in a heaven of excess where the whole world bows down at our feet.

Meanwhile, we can satisfy our appetite with literature about kings and queens and fairy godmothers, watch movies that portray such grandeur of the past and present, and flip television channels to view the lives of the rich and famous.

There is little wrong with being rich, but the mentality of wanting to be rich to acquire power to dominate and control other people and resources to satisfy egocentric fantasies is as problematic, similar to putting a child in charge of a nuclear bomb.

For someone to want more than his or her fair share of any resource, and then go to extremes to obtain it is what can be described as an expression of greed. A number of people, a social or professional group or even an entire society may directly or indirectly get involved in predatory practices under the disguise of doing business. Genuine business is, however, a fair exchange of goods and services at every level, but most of us would be divided on this definition of fairness.

Those of us that are already immersed in the philosophy of ugliness would be most adamant that business can take care of itself and that profits are more important than people. Most businesses, however, involve people, but the fair exchange is always open to question. The fanatic pursuits of business have little or nothing to do with people and everything to do with profits. Its code of ethics dictates a mindset that contradicts with what is propagated in its mission statements in a similar manner that politicians make decisions and take actions based on mitigating circumstances. Those mitigating circumstances in business have more to do with preserving or protecting the business, and increasing profits.

Saying one thing and doing another has become not only acceptable but also fashionable at almost every level of society these days, and there is vested interest in keeping it that way.

NURTURING THE PHILOSOPHY OF OPPOSITES

The crusaders have posted their guardians at every station of human services and need to keep the crusade vibrant, active, and real at all times. If people can get accustomed to things happening a certain way, they can convince themselves that these things are real, and that will be more than half of the battle won. Once people believe that lies are true, they will support all the lies and resist all truths.

The War of Opposites is waged first in our minds, then flows naturally to the rest of the body. It starts with us feeling confident and assured that we are safe and going in the right direction, and that all our needs and wants will be provided for us by the system that we support. Obviously, the platoons are out in force, performing parades and other side-shows on the breakdown lanes to get us to stop, subscribe, and be entertained. It is so easy to design plots and costumes for the side shows because they can build them around our dreams and aspirations, which are based on fantasy and not reality.

We always have something we would like to see happen to make our lives ideal, and that is the open hunting ground where the soldiers from the platoons make up their tactical formations. They do not strike as pirates for what they truly are, but rather invite themselves with our blessing and give us a reason to make them honorary family friends.

The platoons that specialize in headhunting await us to get a breakdown or a blowout in our lane, and decapitate us financially and spiritually with the dragon loans they offer. There are the scavengers who prey upon the poorest and least equipped among us to devour what is left of our enthusiasm after we discover the dilemma of our circumstances. Then comes pouring into the fray the entertainers in all manner of costume and disguises to put on a circus to make us laugh to help us mask the pain or reinterpret the truth to make it more palatable. This platoon will even use the disguise of charity to deflect issues of poverty, using comedy as a pain depressor, and plenty of information to advance the creed of ignorance.

The creed of ignorance is the key weapon that is used to bombard us into heavenly wastelands as they pour from their curriculum dead knowledge and useless skills that intoxicate us with the false pride that we have been adequately educated. We get so saturated with facts and research information, that we feel pride in the volume of facts we have accumulated, not realizing that without the empowering skills to make connections, the education we have received may prove more to be a detriment to us than a savior.

We were supposed to have been educated in a way that prepared us to be able to discern the quality of our education, and to use it to empower ourselves to make changes for our betterment. Instead, we

Our aspirations are now to become excessively rich

were given the kinds of information and
orientation that made us surrender the best of our
capacity and resources as consumables for the
system. Instead of a lifestyle of concern for the
wellbeing of others and action for the improvement
of the community, our aspirations are now to
become excessively rich and isolated from others

except when they can serve us. They have entrenched us into a life of speculation where we hope to one day be able to live beyond our means in the most abnormal and unrealistic of conditions.

SPOILS OF THE WAR OF OPPOSITES

To even aspire to do things that are abnormal gives a close indication of how far we have come to being abnormal. Once we have arrived at that stage of being abnormal, there is no limit to what we can do to fulfill our abnormal urges and ambitions. The worst casualties of any war are those who willingly and happily surrender themselves, fully confident that they are being set loose like vultures into their communities as guardians or ambassadors of ugliness. Driven by the creed of ignorance, they penetrate every level of society, advocating about how edifying it is to be abnormal and how beneficial it is to be ugly. Only those of us who have acquired some influence, power or even wealth will serve as role models to further disorient our communities and young people, until everyone is converted to the new direction of thinking against their innate tendencies and desires of caring for each other.

This is the atmosphere that they say contributes to good business and government. When most people have been repatriated to the new philosophy and organized accordingly, the lieutenants and guardians from the various platoons will emerge as heroes to receive their awards of honor. Somehow, we are just as excited to celebrate them as we do our leaders, politicians, corporations, and social organizations. These are the people who lay the foundations and design the roads on which we travel. They mark the lanes of demarcation to dictate our paths and ambitions.

Ironically, we trust them to reorganize our lives, to take care of our families, enact our laws, and protect us and our futures. Then, suddenly, there are changes in the pattern of traffic. A carpool lane emerges with a bold dividing line that we underlings are not allowed to cross. We can see traffic over there but we have no idea how those people got into that lane, or how we can get over there if we want to join them. They are our leaders and executives who possess a lane of their own.

However, our lanes are starting to merge and get crowded. We have already started to bang into each other, sideswiping and crunching ourselves. Suddenly, we are all bundled together into a pool of travelers building up into a gridlock. Staying

focused now has become a challenge with all kinds of bumps and scrapes occurring along the way. There is nepotism, racism, discrimination and, of course, all kinds of corruption and exploitation.

In this clutter of circumstances, life can become like a business when we have to negotiate a lane of our own to move ahead in traffic. In our desperation, we are unable to flow over to the carpool lane since the bold lines have transformed gradually into a solid curb, then into a wall that grows in height and width. Escaping into the carpool lane has now become impossible.

THE WAR INTENSIFIES

The war against nature has now become intensified. Pitted against each other with no escape to a carpool lane of our own, we can resort to all manner of maneuvers to survive. The tactics we use to maneuver ourselves are laden with pitfalls or potholes, into which we will eventually fall as victims of our own schemes and shortcomings. When too many of us are engaged in unwholesome competition for survival, we can create a bigoted ecosystem. This gridlock may develop its own heat and humidity, like the famine conditions of an arid desert, parching our constitutions and testing our morale.

Under the intense heat of the gridlock, some of us can begin to see mirages of our secret desires, which create heavenly gardens and waterfalls out of the quicksand and dangerous cliffs that await us. When the ingredient of the self is injected into the circumstances of gridlock, we can get lost in the side lanes or exits, pursuing the ghosts of our narrow minded dreams. We should be mindful of what we secretly wish in our hearts, for the heat of a gridlock can drive us beyond our true character, and make us behave in the most unusual manner.

Under these circumstances, the philosophy of ugliness rules supreme, as we surrender our better human qualities to the forces of discrimination, substance abuse, lasciviousness, and all manners of predatory practices. Some of us may never find our way back onto the main highway; instead we end up taking comfort in a false illusion that may prove to be a feasible alternative to the gridlock.

However, the perpetrators of the War of Opposites may have organized their skirmishes to accommodate our every frustration. When we resort to these desperate displays of raw self-confidence, we fail to realize that we are dispersing toward traps that have already been set in anticipation of our reactions. Instead of relying on our natural abilities and inclinations, we resort to depending on all kinds of illusions that have been conveniently injected into our thinking and believing.

Our improvised ecosystem has made it necessary for us to have them to inoculate us from our fears and anxieties. Our raw confidence is based on the availability of these illusions to effectively mask the symptoms, illnesses, and aftereffects. They do not refer to the causes, since that would restore us to a sense of reason that would defeat their purpose.

The platoons are specifically divided according to rank and purpose. It is natural that when we divorce ourselves from nature we will become ill, so they prove their manmade substitute or illusions of comfort in drugs and therapies. Where health and wellness is concerned, the War of Opposites is focused on sickness maintenance. Once a victim has crossed the line and becomes ill, they are hooked up to drugs and therapy for the rest of their lives. Since drugs and therapies come at a price, it is more economically feasible to deal with them in isolation and to refer to them in specific terms.

There are experts to advise and diagnose treatments for psychological maladjustments. They, too, make certain that the entrance is sealed when they apply the drugs of the mind and we accept ourselves for what we are diagnosed to be. There are systems in place to accommodate us all, with expansions that are as limitless as the bottomless pit in which we find ourselves. There are hospitals like cities and therapeutic centers mushrooming all around them to guarantee that all our needs are provided for once we cross the borderline.

COUNTER OFFENSIVES

The worst setback to the crusade in the War of Opposites is holistic education that takes us back to where we belong with nature. That is why the struggle is so intense at the level of ideologies and beliefs. By choosing to ignore traditional practices and norms, the crusaders peddle theories about how to enhance nature with their substitutes and extensions. They must convince us that they are operating from a thorough understanding of nature to help it to provide us with its maximum benefits. They are out to prove that the substitutes and improvisations they provide are better and safer than what nature itself provides. They can manufacture fake food in laboratories to look and taste like real food.

What is impressive to the eyes
may not be as compatible,
nutritious and safe for the body.

Technology which has been advanced to afford us time and better access to information and to each other has dominated us instead, overwhelming us with too much of the wrong kinds of ingredients. It has narrowed the discrepancy between fantasy and reality right at our fingertips, creating a pseudo-culture in our minds that is just an extension of our imagination.

Reality is now fantasy within the realm of the technology

The physical flexibilities and agilities we need in our everyday lives we can execute through virtual reality computer games on our Xbox control systems. Somehow we seem content to remain as couch potatoes while our computer or film characters are busy doing everything we could be doing ourselves. Reality is now fantasy within the realm of the technology within our reach and under our control. We can now do more than was ever thought possible with our imagination through technology, yet we do much less with ourselves, and for the betterment of our true character.

Technology has created doors of opportunities that enable us to interact and connect with each other, but more often we use it instead to isolate ourselves and become more preoccupied with the technology itself. Once it gets grounded deeply into our subconscious, technology becomes the magic genie to whom we will make our wishes. These desires almost always include getting ahead of our neighbor, peeking into his or her privacy, coveting his or her treasures and personal resources, or depriving him or her of the just deserve to his or her efforts.

The more opportunities we have to freely express ourselves, the more we use those opportunities to restrict ourselves from the rest of the world. If we must include the world, it has to be from a distance away from us, as we communicate and reason through statistics and polls.

In order to truly reach out to other human beings, we first have to view others from the same level of consciousness that we view ourselves. For those who have not yet graduated from egocentrism, that can become impossible to do, because big issues affecting masses of people become reduced in our minds compared to how we feel ourselves. Nature does not have a choice but to evolve, change and grow in the unending cycle of metamorphosis. We are the only specimen from nature that can control that choice from within. While our bodies grow and we gain more experience and insight, we can choose to narrow our vision and responsibilities, and remain in a form of intellectual infancy.

These limitations pervade among us as individuals, and can prevail to spread like a cancer to produce the conflicts that we have come to accept as inevitable or even normal in general society today. The force that is internal controls and enhances the forces that are external, giving them legitimacy to act and give purpose to the things we do in our lives. That is why the crusaders of the War of Opposites try to get as close as possible, to win our confidence and assure us that we are on the right track with them.

Illusions like these attract us to the temporary pleasures of the philosophy of ugliness that always reinforce the aggrandizement of the self. We make ourselves slaves and victims of the conflicts we harbor within our minds because we are reluctant to release our true selves from their encasements.

There is this region on the highway of our lives where all the lanes seem to merge and lead to Paradoxia, the big entertainment city, with all the casinos and games and the Egotopia hotels and apartments. It is the widest exit in the journey of life that has more lanes than when we first started. It gives the impression that the end of the highway has come, and that anywhere else after that is not worth traveling.

We get lost in the maze of Paradoxia

THE CITY OF PARADOXIA

Once we enter the city of Paradoxia, we almost never get out since there is so much to do on so many winding roads that we can forget that we are on a journey to somewhere else. We get lost in the maze, because the end of one loop is the beginning of another, and we get increasingly mesmerized with the Ferris wheels of lifestyles we are attempting to explore. It becomes difficult to even think about the exit because the winding roads take us further away from it.

This is the main city of the Haven of Opposites for which all the wars are being fought, and where all the spoils of war are sent to furnish it with monuments. These are the lanes in which we can get obsessed with analogies and ideologies, beliefs and customs that create a fog that blinds our vision, forcing a compromise to who we are. In these lanes, the discrepancy narrows between reality and belief, self and others, truth and untruth, going forward or stepping backward.

In those lanes, our system of logics reason in the reverse so that we find it perfectly normal to interpret and act upon life situations with expectations that suit our reverse way of thinking. The pursuit of peace, for example, may be the only solution of war, but we support and propagate the expansion of war. Here, we want everything for ourselves, but somehow we are failing to recognize that there are people out there just like us, waiting for us to give into the pool of life so that there is enough for us all.

We know that love is the solution to all manners of hate, yet we cannot help but love ourselves and our own more. This gives us the basis to hate everything and everyone that is different from us. We are so confident about the untruth that we tell ourselves that we would put our integrity on the line to defend it as the truth.

When we are beset with the complexity of Paradoxia, we cannot help but become paranoid and seek a support system from which to operate to give legitimacy and integrity to our actions and beliefs. To sanction and anoint ourselves, we incriminate others through clubs, organizations, and agencies of all types to camouflage our true intentions. Once we are headed in the direction of Paradoxia, the lanes become blocked with solid lines that prevent us from coming out of our commitment. We become proficient at using the qualities of love to promote hate, and those of peace to make war. We become so much a part of the intrigues of our lifestyles, that our minds become conditioned to this Ferris wheel pattern of living. Very soon we get lost and we try to convince ourselves that we are not, especially when the luxuries, neon lights, and games demand the price for their benefits, and we have drained ourselves of our resources to pay.

When we become overwhelmed by our indulgences and our constitutions begin to weaken from lack of resolve, we surrender to denial to persuade ourselves that we are happy and satisfied. When obsessions run amok in the paradox of opposites, they reveal themselves through beliefs that we hold very dear. The road or the journey in life ceases to matter at this stage. It is the beliefs and the mirages of our obsession that become real and bigger than we are. Then we end up with cult systems in our heads that entirely change our style and purpose of living.

A storm is nothing more than a normal occurrence of nature

BENEFITS OF THE STORM

Way up ahead, a storm has been brewing, if we have the insight to see it through the windshield of the fantasy lifestyle. It may be a tornado, or a heavy rainstorm, but the distinction would not matter if we still had the ability to discern the aesthetics of a setting sun. It need not be viewed as the impending downpour of consequences for our shortcomings and misgivings, but rather the process that tests the system for cracks and inconsistencies.

It could be that our lifestyle encourages the stagnation of will power and the Pygmalion effect that produces the restlessness and insecurity we feel at every turn. A storm is nothing more than a normal occurrence of nature that has its cycles, similar to the crises that ripen in our lives during certain periods of our growth. Once all systems are in working order, we can survive the course of events and even reap their benefits. There are always ample warning signs if we choose to see them, and not get blinded by self-denial instead.

The storms that visit in the course of our journey are nearly always blessings in disguise that can shower down abundant resources, helping us to reshape our destiny for our next life phase. It may be just the showers we need for the seeds we have planted for the scheduled harvest of our many ambitions. Every storm has an aesthetic of its own, even when it is raging with turbulence and fury. In life, everything is relative, even when it appears contradictory. The fast can be outrun by the slow, the soft can penetrate the hard, and the hot can be subdued by the cold.

We need the most turbulent of life circumstances to awaken us from the drunken stupor of complacency and self-conceit. It is the worst that brings out the best; the greatest trials and tragedies never fail to produce our heroes. Out of the storm will emerge our philosophers, our humanists and our model politicians who will bring us back to an era of peaceful consciousness.

Stormy days are the best to test our resolve for everything both big and small, our beliefs and heartfelt convictions. That is what tests our true mettle for being human, for animals are blessed with only the instinct to respond to what they do not necessarily understand as we do. They internalize and process with their whole being, then act according to the laws of nature. They are aware of their obligations and benefits, and yield to their limitations.

Observe what an animal, bird, or bug does prior to, during or after a storm, and we can compile a catalog of hints for storm readiness.

They are very aware of the cycles of nature and where their very existence and survival fits into the pattern of things around them. They do not panic, as we do; they just calmly and deliberately act. They do not run hysterically; they get out of the way long before nature claims that space to do its work. For most animals, they can hardly wait to return to benefit from what nature has done for them. I agree that we do not share the same needs as animals, but we certainly do share the same predicament in our common existence with nature.

ANIMAL RESPONSE TO THE STORM

How is it then that animals, who are less equipped than humans, seem to respond better to the crises in their lives than we respond to ours? A storm of nature is a storm for all, but every living species faces a crises of its own that are equivalent to storms. The difference between us and all other species is that while they conform and adapt to the patterns and processes of nature, we as humans keep striving to contain and control those patterns and processes to suit our whims and fancies.

Of course, we pretentiously say that we learn about the weather so that we can make predictions for our safety. It seems to be within our nature to start with an honorable, innocent intention, only to graduate to hideous, destructive, and dishonorable ones.

The storms that herald the crises of our lives are naturally those of our own making; it is the fermentation of ingredients we express through the ways that we think, act and relate to each other as human beings. We are a privileged species in that we have choices, but we exercise that privilege to the extreme, even to our own detriment. No other species enjoys this privilege.

Their response is registered in their genes, which easily enables them to act in unison with a single purpose. Those that do not conform perish, since there is no other means of self-fulfillment or survival but through the world of their own kind. Humans have become too laid back and with their choice capabilities, so much so that we seem to gravitate more readily to choices that bring pain and suffering to our own kind. These choices are made mainly because of social cues that have led us to believe it is logical or politically correct to do so.

Nature is tempered with discretion and will not outperform itself or function beyond the borders of its jurisdiction.

It will stop once it has run its course and fulfilled its obligations. It will not discriminate and does not exhibit the tendency to target specific area, objects or persons based on egocentric motives. It is too preoccupied with its mission to renew, refresh, replenish, and improve.

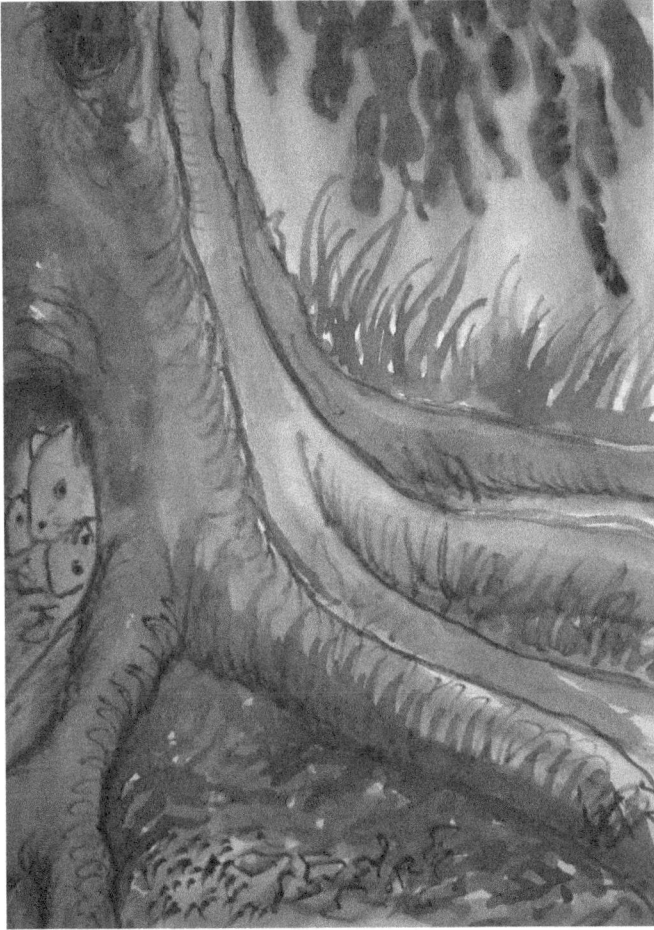

**Animals and insects do not have to comprehend the concept
of a storm**

HUMAN RESPONSES TO THE STORM

Animals and insects do not have to comprehend the concept of a storm. They simply respond to it as an opportunity to synchronize with the next cycle of their existence or obligation. They hold no grudges because they are not capable of such things, so preoccupied are they with responding to opportunities to recreate themselves through the rhythm of the cycles of their environment. We humans are a peculiar exception, since we harbor in our deepest subconscious concepts and vocabularies that reinforce the negative energies we inculcate into our lives.

We are persistent in engineering storms among ourselves and show little discretion in the methods we use to target special groups of people that do not conform to our egocentric expectations. We have our own vocabulary that allows us to condone the cycles of destruction we create in our paths. Collectively we call it politics or commerce or even religion when we have to, so that we can justify our actions and intentions as we destroy, commit atrocities, and leave nothing less than famine and depression in our paths. We seem to cherish the nurturing of human conflict in our societies, using our power to shape the destiny of others to suit our egocentric aspirations.

Too many of our systems are built to work progressively against themselves and the people for whom they are designed. If they include an element of betterment and improvement, it is nearly always based on the guarantee that some particular group of persons will never benefit. The storms that hover like huge dark clouds over human existence represent the conflicts that prevail between our faulty beliefs and how to choose to relate to each other.

When we defy the natural, we facilitate the unnatural and have no alternative but to conform to and abide by its consequences.

When we absorb into our systems ingredients that are inconsistent with our nature, the discomfort that follows is only part of the greater pain that will follow in the process of our readjustment. Restraining the talent, expressions, and opportunities of others because of their ethnicity or beliefs puts ourselves in that very same restriction. We are the victims of our own negative thinking in the same way that we produce victims from the negative conditions we create.

During our everyday personal and public lives, we project the elements of what will determine the kinds of responses we are likely to make during the storms in our lives. Our response is a reflection of the concepts we have nurtured and the philosophies we have adopted. We may choose to sincerely conform to our inner convictions to do what feels natural, uplifting and invigorating, by using the storms to renew and refresh ourselves and those around us. Otherwise, we have no alternative but to seek shelter from the ominous thunder and lightning erupting in our minds, producing conditions that are far more violent than those most intense in nature.

Impending retribution can force us into a state of chronic paranoia, forcing even more victims to shelter themselves from the storms that perpetually plague us in our minds. When we feel guilty of violating our better nature through the things we do to others, the emptiness that persists can produce the illusion of a devastating storm that is nothing more than a reflection of our conscience. That is when we seek shelter under a philosophy or ideology to deflect our fears of impending consequences. Even governments employ systems and machineries to detract from this surging fear, engaging the manipulation of circumstances against their sea of crimes and neglect and of duty.

Such governments are forced to constantly reinforce their levies against a mounting surge of protests and oppositions. When there is no freedom to distort, there is a need to control and suppress. When we dominate others and overwhelm them with our demands, they learn to detest our presence and avoid us as much as possible. We may even clutter our minds with petty intrigues to either service our schemes of self-aggrandizement or envy, or wage personal wars within ourselves at the expense of others. The dust that blurs our vision most likely is the pollution we have developed through neglecting our obligation to contribute when the need to do so came our way.

Instead, we waited around to complain, spreading the blame around to everyone but ourselves when we had the first real opportunity to fix or address the issue. We have every reason to be concerned for our safety and peace of mind from the eye of the storm; since it was generated by us, it will subsequently return to us. It may not be that easy to try to convince ourselves that the storm is a distant phenomenon that is not connected to us and therefore is not within our power to change.

However, our denial is but an effort to escape our involvement by commission or omission. Our lack of engagement contributes to the scale of events swinging in the current direction, confirming our silent consent. Now that the consequences of our denial have become more apparent and visible, we strive instead to sanctify ourselves by circumventing the issues that plague us.

THE STORM WITHIN A RELATIONSHIP

When we, as partner or passenger, are in such denial of the outcome of our actions, the storm rages within and around us as we continue to negotiate the impassible ravines and treacherous cliffs on a typical calm and sunny day. The wars we fight within are perpetual bombardments, secret prejudices and desires that prey on our peace of mind.

In this perpetual state of anxiety, we are likely to lose our rhythm with our partner and the role they are anxious to play to complement us in our struggle for survival. Partners' lives are originally supposed to harbor one vision, but when dominated with selfish resorts of desperation each partner can develop the aspiration to travel in his or her own lane. If our partner secedes to give us the authority at the helm, it is because he or she felt invested in the mission of our lives together, with the interest of the siblings in mind. That is the authority that gets usurped for the cause of one's self and the single pursuits of one's exploits, struggles, and satisfaction.

Our partner has to endure the role of chief spectator to be dragged helplessly through the jungles of our desperation and used as bait for the predators of our misconceptions and misplaced desires.

The storms in the relationship started brewing within the compartments of the sanctuary we once shared long before the roof started leaking. The assurance of feeling at home had long been lost or forgotten, leaving just a shell of our former selves to remain as a stoic monument of the past.

Our partner was sitting in the front with us, surviving the shrapnel and the fumes, the blows that pierced and shoved at us, and with windshield wipers that only worked when we wanted them to justify our actions and decisions. Our partner had sat there, transforming day after day, moment after moment, improvising on the sanctuary and the philosophy that used to be, to find ways to exist on his or her own terms. The days were long and the nights were even longer. They may have felt dragged throughout the journey, and tossed around according to our own whims. They had survived the relationship by assuming that they were in the place they were supposed to be.

While we were busy fighting our own cold wars and focusing on the storms, our partner was stuck repairing the umbrellas that were constantly being blown away, and finding excuses to defend philosophies and decisions that they did not quite understand. They had eventually stopped belonging to the relationship, but they needed to be with someone until they could truly find themselves again, and learn to own something of their own. We had not noticed this predicament as we steered our ego-fueled carousel. There is something about a carousel that makes you want to ride it, even though you know that it leads to nowhere.

Perhaps it is the thrill of the ride itself, or perhaps sharing the ride makes it seem more authentic or legitimate that we are going somewhere. So, our partners awaken from this carousel dream to try to reposition or reorganize themselves. If we are not careful we may forget to remember our copilot on the right. We can get so lost in navigating our ego trips that our partners can easily blend into our blind spot, after being left so far behind in the front seat of our lives.

Children in the backseat are getting a comprehensive view of us and the models we portray

VIEW TO THE BACK SEAT

Meanwhile, the children in the backseat are getting a comprehensive view of both of us and the models we portray. They had no choice but to be where we had put them, but the lane that we had travelled provided bumps and turns that got their attention. They had lived through the twists of the dramas we had created, and now are at a point of decision due to the forces that have shaped their minds. For them it was not always easy to sit back and adapt, especially when leaning forward was always uncomfortable and even painful.

Like our partnerships, they have come to realize that love can produce the most painful of compromises, so they lean more heavily onto the partner closer to them to access the comforts and understanding that is compatible with their needs. They know that we were too preoccupied with our own problems to truly cater to their needs. They had tolerated us during their Spring season with picnic feasts that generally drowned their reason and temporarily distracted them from the missteps that we had made.

Summer had developed sufficient enough heat in the backseat to prompt them to take notice of their condition from the wear and tear of the journey. They would prefer to think that they have not given up on us, but now they look forward to the rest stop to breathe some fresher air of their own. The heat flowed toward the back seat and produced mirages of a better world that were as narrow as the space we gave them. They looked forward to a world they had come to know through needs and aspirations which fostered them while traveling in a lane they never knew or understood.

It was not their journey and could not have been their lane, but we made them travel it anyway, under our terms and conditions. They had seen the sideshows and parades along the way, and yet they struggled to keep pace with our every move. They wished we had driven faster, to outpace the many dangers that pursued us along the way.

To a child, there is nothing more frightening than demons disguised as angels emerging from their imagination at every turn, perfect mirages from heated desires that get stronger along the way. We tucked them away safely to be available for our own convenience when we needed to perform our rituals at their expense. We strived to give the love they knew not, so preoccupied they were dealing with their panic; so to them, falsehoods become truths and truths become falsehoods. They knew that what we had struggled to provide never really reached them or their hearts. They felt the emptiness of feeding on wind and hope, that one day things will get better.

To a child, there is nothing more frightening than demons disguised as angels

From our world, we had done all we could to stock the pantry with our best intentions, but we had kept the keys in the pockets of our hearts. Our children may be products of circumstances, or they may be the gateway to another level of existence, first with ourselves and then with the rest of the world. They are our second chance to review our own lives, to refine our spirits and redefine our philosophy of who we are and what we really want to be. We need them to rediscover our inner selves.

That is why it is easy to look beyond them back to ourselves and not realize how much we have disenfranchised them with our egotistic ambitions.

To love them, we will have to extend ourselves beyond our illusions and ambitions to connect to them for who and what they are. Instead, we may be trying to connect them to who and what we are, so that we can manipulate their existence to suit our ambitions and fancies. Our relationships with our children, therefore, may be based on mixed signals of communication in which neither party is enjoying the real value of each other's existence. They could be saying things to each other that they could never mean, based on their level of awareness. The word love, for example, more readily escapes the lips of someone who aspires to be loved, when he or she is not yet capable of defining what it means.

Of course, we can all assure ourselves that we can define what we mean by what we say. Of course, we can sum up all our intelligence and resources to defend our pride. We can circumvent our misunderstandings by resorting to technical, or social definitions that provide opportunities for fluid combinations of words to meet our needs. The truth, however, is in the conviction. The harder we have to try to convince ourselves and anyone else, the less we understand what we are really trying to explain.

DEFINING LOVE IN THE JOURNEY OF PARENTHOOD

Where love is concerned, true conviction comes from the heart. It is very possible to exist in the same space with persons we are supposed to love and not know that we do not love them. We may even preoccupy ourselves with routines and rituals to persuade ourselves and others outwardly that we are connected and engaged when in fact we are not. I suspect that love is too high a requirement when we have so many priorities to fulfill the dramatic aspirations that dominate our lives. It would be convenient to assume that these priorities are mere distractions imposing themselves upon our true intentions to do what is inherently compulsory.

However, the paradigm on which we operate in our thinking influences the choices we make, so that the priorities we adopt are, therefore, not accidental. We subconsciously or unconsciously operate from the paradigm of our personality and make those choices accordingly because that is who and what we are.

Our innate nature is based on the internal, to value and connect with all things that are natural: our partner, offspring, our home and that special place in our lives. It is the internal that makes life rich and meaningful; all the externals are mere frivolities on which the internal thrives or stifles.

When we shift our focus to the external, and our choices in life are all based on the frivolous, our lives become a platform for conflict and confusion. When we get preoccupied with the culture of excess, the corresponding rituals that eventually clutter our lives are not mere distractions but rather reflections of what we have become internally. They are ghosts of the shadows of the light that once burned within. The direction in which we were going caused us to miss our children along the way, even as we harbored them in the back seat of our lives.

They had been part of the excess of external living we had pursued. We could not connect with them on the inside because we had been living on the outside, using materials we had acquired along the way to bribe and pacify them into accepting their condition. Our offspring may actually have been at home in the prison of their minds and were never able to connect with their captors. They needed to learn to grow into their space, their home and experiences in order to connect with us. A home is not necessarily defined by its physical characteristics or dimensions. It is the emotional, spiritual, and personal meanings that it invokes on the inside that matters most.

What goes on in a home among children and their parents is more than just bodies shifting in space and sharing conversations. Conversations are not merely an exchange of words or ideas, but rather an interaction of impulses. When we get preoccupied with the material excess on the outside, we fail to connect on the inside and hardly become aware that we are communicating with our children unwholesomely. We have no choice because even they had become a part of the empire of materialism we had built around us.

They had long ceased to be the priority they ought to have been. Instead of guiding them to embrace a worthwhile future, we used them as instruments to justify our past. How can we connect with our children just an arm's length from our reach, when we are panicked, fleeing ghosts of our misdeeds and indiscretions, or are busy parading in a bandwagon of glory and ambition at their expense? No wonder we have gotten more efficient in establishing a façade to complement everything that is genuine and real, so that we can maintain our privileges on the materialistic outside.

Even our children were among this imposing establishment against the inside. The roller coaster culture of childrearing is set within a system of avoidance that can engineer excitements and dramas of its own, many plagued with double signals to the children who are perpetually taken for the ride. What about the parties, graduations, fancy trips, and extravagant gifts that are nothing more than efforts to gain public recognition for what we do not deserve?

From within the containment of narrow parental upbringing, they can unfold like a flower does

Our children can be waved like banners to establish our status in the face of society, and paraded around like specimens to help us stage our various agendas. If we could realize the dilemma of a child stuck in the backseat with no way out, we would probably be more inclined to let in more fresh air. Yet, from within the containment of narrow parental upbringing, they can unfold like a flower to the sun, radiating their better qualities that attract the events and circumstances to fertilize them to the next level of their existence and purpose in life, beyond what their parents can ever hope to teach them.

The back seat is still the best view to interact with history and speculate on a future. Children can choose to mimic their parents at the wheel while waiting for their own journey to begin. Only seeing through the eyes of our parents is like staying in the cocoon stage of our lives and not graduating to the fullest of our potential.

When the process of youth has run its course, we begin to be original and to unfold from the cocoon to a less simplistic view of life. By being original, we hold a unique view or side of the prism that holds the key to solving the mysteries of the universe we all share.

From the backseat, our children have the strategic advantage to explore the realities of life through play. That process must run its course and the cocoon of youth and innocence needs to crack to release the genius or the demon that they want to or have chosen to be. The time will soon come when we will reach the rest stop to release ourselves to the next level of our existence.

WINTER – THE REST STOP

When we all descend upon the rest stop, all of us will have arrived at different junctions of our journey. For our children, it is just about Spring and they are anxious to launch into the world to explore all of their possibilities. Those who have already plowed through the avenues of life can easily be tempted to concede to all manner of limitations because that is how they have been programmed.

For some people, the journey has never been theirs; for they have become passengers waiting to be deposited to assume a journey dictated for them. For them, there is no end but a beginning, an assumption to the struggles or challenges to which they had been introduced. The end is always linked to a beginning, and the beginning determines the end. It is at the rest stop that we can begin to find how our personality casts a unique tint to the way we choose to look at things. Our children have the natural inclination to view everything from the beginning where they started, where they sampled the journey of life from the back seat. The initial impression, the intuition, the inspiration or the exposure will texture the surface on which their lives will run.

When we all disembark to reflect on and review our lives, we will indulge in pure projections of what we would like to be and do based on the illusions of what we had learned from the back seat of our youthful days. The confidence and assurances to which we have matured mix with ease, as does illusion with reality from which we build dreams and aspirations to carve a destiny of our own. We all eventually find ourselves at the rest stop, each with a different mission and purpose, although we may not recognize or admit it.

THE HAZARDS OF LOVING

For some of us, that winter rest stop may be the first time that we take stock of our lives after plowing through in pursuit of temporary pleasures that are now becoming frozen from the coldness that is fast approaching. Our children may have long lost the connection of what kept them secure and content in their places in our backseats, and will therefore not be inclined to wait for the fulfillment of what is meaningful to us. They explore the rest stop for an exit, and to find resources to sustain them on their own journey, in the same manner we had done when we first started. It takes a whole life's journey to reach this point of our lives, but the more we try to gather of what we had gained, the less we seem to find. It seems that what we have grasped and cherished most along our journey are trophies of what we had lost along the way.

They do not glitter now as they used to. Instead,

they seem to crumble with just a glance or touch, and there is no way we can contain them to give a sense of purpose to our intentions and the struggles we have endured to obtain them. Before we take the exit to continue on our journey, we need to redefine the very things our whole life has embraced, even the very reason why we chose the lane in which we travelled. At the rest stop, everyone is reviewing his or her options, so we have no alternative but to review ours.

For some reason, our partner may disembark for the rest stop as readily as our children, and may seem somewhat detached while doing it. It can leave us wondering whether it was an occasion that he or she had been looking forward to. The rhythm of the relationship may have been slipping on the gears, especially further along the journey. While the engine of our communication should have been cruising easily at higher speeds, for some reason the usual mundane issues would be as difficult as going uphill. It is no wonder that the rest stop brings such great relief to both partners. Living within something fearful is more fearful than the fear itself, especially when that fear is linked to the love we nurtured for our partner. Love, however, is only pure when it is natural and uncontaminated, and reciprocal between two partners.

Life's journeys are laden with infections along the way, especially according to the lane that is travelled. All exposures that are unnatural, or manmade are potential contaminants, depending on how and when they bestow themselves. Our lifestyle and philosophy are the vents through which they can penetrate our lives to eventually distort our focus and our relationship with our partner and our children. That is how it is so easy to lose our children along the way, to predators of all descriptions lurking hungrily at every turn in the course of our journey. They are content to engage us in increments when our connection is strong, and we are likely to think as one.

However, what each one of us sees through the windshield of life can be different, or even radically transformed in the windows of our minds as we journey the treacherous highways. In some cases, our partner brings us there, perhaps out of curiosity or neglect, but mainly because we may have deserted the sanctuary of our love and trust for each other. At the rest stop we may come to the realization that things were not what they seemed and that fantasy and reality are like neon lights trading places in electric flashes along the way. We may have taken it for granted that our partner initially gave us the role as driver, so they could be our copilot in the passenger front seat. The flips, thrills and intrigues we might have sent them through might have long disenchanted them from the virtues of the partnership. Physically, they may be going through the motions of the responsibilities and commitments, but in the mind they may have long resorted to waiting patiently for the rest stop to disembark. For them, the rest stop provides an opportunity to recuperate and reestablish what is left of their self-esteem.

Now it is more likely that they will resort to measures to save their faces and their pride. When we do not live within the paradigms of our true nature, we become forces to distort the functions of other platforms such as politics, law, religion, and even spirituality to try to create the illusion of balance in our lives. The sanctuary of our relationship to our partner and our children may have been left open and exposed to the vicious elements that we had condoned for too long in our interaction with each other. So parched and crisp its walls have become, that they are ready to ignite, to consume what is left of the façade for the dignity that it once boasted. What would normally have been viewed as a tragedy, transforms itself into a virtue at the rest stop.

FINDING OURSELVES AGAIN

Suddenly, we are forced to reacquaint ourselves with our purpose from the beginning of the journey we had started, with the dreams and aspirations that fueled our efforts along the way. Somehow, it seems that it is the beginning that determines the end. It seems so inconsistent and blatantly ironic that after we have managed traveling on our journey this far, we can discover that we can become lost along the way.

Getting lost is a predicament that is a traveler's nightmare, especially when the traveler suspects that he or she is closer to the destination. Finding ourselves in such a predicament could arouse paranoia that there are predators all around us. For many of us, the world we leave behind can appear to be a labyrinth, seeking to overtake and imprison us in its entrails. If we dare to look hard and long enough, what we once viewed as accomplishments and victory over circumstances can gradually transform into stairways of regret and bitter remorse.

There was a time when our partners used to dream up thousands of different ways to please us and make us happy, then dedicate themselves to the mission to fulfill them one by one. Now at the rest stop, our partner may want to explore new prospects for existence beyond the sanctuary. The tenderness, the courtesies and the heavenly gestures of Summer can rapidly fade like a dream once the dew and fog has cleared. There lie the bare bones of reality, the skeletons of our misdeeds and poor decisions, the thorns of retributions of the path we had taken and the life we had lived. There is a level of protection we can enjoy for staying with a partner from whatever residue is left from the sanctuary of the relationship. Never mind that our confidence and composure is shaken and the ghosts of our fears can begin to pounce on us from every side. There is always hope to rekindle a relationship that had a great beginning.

Physically, they have drifted apart

Jealousy can work miracles on our psyche, forcing us to recognize what we have missed during the routines and rituals of our relationship. The loss of a partner and the decline of the relationship has first and foremost to do with the spirit. If we are not paying attention, we can be shocked to discover that, although we can be close in proximity of each other physically, we can be miles apart mentally and spiritually.

A train does not leave its rails without making a noisy, thunderous rattle on the tracks to the inconvenience and discomfort of everyone within the carriages. When we are obsessed with our egocentric pursuits, we are usually deaf and blind to the inferences of the disturbance around us, except when it embraces or disturbs the priorities of our world. How, therefore, can we know when our partner is drifting away in the spirit, when our main concern is their physical presence and attributes to endear our aspirations.

Not realizing when our partner has drifted to the edge of desperation is a clear indication of how lost we ourselves were. There is no greater feeling of desperation we can have than when we are lost in the spirit. It is only when we grow out of our egotism that we begin to realize the blind paths that we had been cutting. Our partner with whom we had cherished a sanctuary can be dragged along through the pathways, only to be entangled in the labyrinth of a lifestyle shaped by us. Our partner's loyalty could either be challenged for growth and refinement or expended through abuse and ruthless scrutiny. It may have been out of loyalty that they have come this far, but blind loyalty for the wrong purpose and for a person heading in the wrong direction is equivalent to a silent conspiracy to assassinate oneself.

When we feel lost, our first reaction to our feelings of panic is to think of predators. To divert from the mainstream of our natural selves is to cut blind paths out of life's circumstances to satisfy our whims and fancies. A partner may feel trapped in their commitment as the path to nowhere continues to open new challenges and temptations that take a piece of our good nature every time we stumble upon a crisis.

THE POSSIBLE VIRTUE OF A CRISIS

Crises are great opportunities for enrichment and growth, but they can affect persons of weak character negatively, creating circumstances that can bring out the worst in people. Exposing our partners unnecessarily to situations where predator influences can torment and have a feast of their good intentions is one way to dis-acknowledge the value of their loyalty and faithful commitment.

In a jungle full of predators, we need
to focus, and not be distracted by
feeling deserted or rejected.

The path that we cut blindly is our way back home, and the philosophy of opposites that had driven us into this maze will provide the secret thread to guide our way back out. It is our obligation to dissuade or even protect our partner from using what is left of his or her spirit to cut deeper tracks from the very blind tracks we had created.

The grass certainly smells fresh and green when we cut it ourselves, and it does boost our spirit with self-esteem to convince ourselves that we are able to take charge and give shape to our own destiny. Our destiny is, however, channeled from the route through which we came, regardless of how far we have strayed and under what circumstances. The rest stop is the most opportune time to revisit and renew our obligations with our partner and to retrace backwards to find our way back to ourselves and the sanctuary to which we belong.

Predators rely heavily for their sustenance on stragglers who get lost

Predators rely heavily for their sustenance on stragglers who get lost and who are too proud and obstinate to admit it. It is the straggler who often brings himself or herself to the predator for a feast under the false assurance that there are new paths towards a sanctuary of his or her own. Paths that begin from pathways of the lost are penetrating deeper into lost territory and are most likely to be infested with traps of betrayal and precipices of false promises. The wind blows the sweet tune of necromancy and the tongues of hypocrites paint a radiant picture of heavenly bliss. That is not the place to leave our partner when we decide to retrace our steps back to where we belong.

Obviously, a distracted partner, overcome with the novelty of their newfound confidence and freedom, may already be entrapped by the demon of his or her own speculation that there is a bed of roses he or she is headed to find. It will not be easy to persuade a jilted or disenchanted partner whose self-esteem and assurance in the sanctuary has long been torn to shreds. Yet our obligation goes beyond the level of pure persuasion to the commitment of guiding our partner back to the awareness of the original self.

Their overindulgence in the politics of accommodating us and our egocentric world of intrigues and self-indulgence had enticed them into their world of wishful thinking. We owe it to ourselves never to leave a partner behind to become counted among the spoils of war. The sense of urgency may add to the retribution we may have to endure, but we have to persevere in our efforts to free our partner from the clutches of an illusion resulting from a bad dream. To those of us that are seasoned through the courses of travel, time develops a special meaning.

FINDING BACK OURSELVES

Based on our experience and our level of maturity, the rest stop makes its demands based on the phase or stage of our growth. We can hardly escape the compulsion to bring some closure to the aspirations we have pursued and the lanes we have traveled throughout our journey. The closure is reflected in the relationship we have with ourselves, our partner, our offspring, and everyone with whom we come into contact. To initiate that level of interaction with ourselves, we need to first come out of ourselves, and deal with our egos and pride as additions to our personality that can prevent us from being our true natural selves. Our interaction with anyone else, including our partner, is limited only by our ability to communicate with ourselves.

As we get more entangled in the philosophy of opposites, we tend to lose contact with ourselves. To hear others, we must first learn how to hear ourselves. Yet the agents of the philosophy of opposites saturate our world with noisy frivolities and sensational toys to keep us from hearing or seeing ourselves and others. We get so very busy with the toys and the cheap pleasures they provide, that we tend to build the purpose of our lives around them, so that everything else has to be adapted to suit our toys. The make-believe life of toys may be appropriate in Spring, but fantasy cannot take the place of reality. Our obsession with materialism and political and social power are but illusions that are more suited to the juvenile world.

Before we attempt to persuade and save our partner, we must first be able to redeem ourselves by acquiring the tools and the awareness. It was the reason why we had lost them in the first place because we had originally lost ourselves. The meaning and purpose of community is either lost or found in our very hearts by the manner in which we interact with those immediately around us.

Those in close proximity, such as our partner and our children, are the windows through which we have the opportunity to view the world. They are the beginning of the journey of discovering ourselves and our true purpose in life. Community has little or nothing to do with things and toys; it has to do with people and how we are able to contribute to the improvement of their lives.

Community begins with the person next to you, and extends infinitely to the furthest reach beyond our vision or comprehension. We limit and restrict ourselves and our potentials according to how we limit our responses to our community and its needs.

Our partner is not merely an extension of our world as we may have been led to believe, but actually is part of our world. Their destiny and life circumstances harbor the same ingredients for success or failure as we would wish for ourselves. Yet we often mislead ourselves into thinking that we are doing our partner or a brother or sister a favor when we extend ourselves for their good. We must realize that our priorities and obligations gradually change the further we go along our journey. The noises and excitements of travel seem to possess less of a charm now that we are getting close to the conclusion of our journey. We have seen and heard it all, but what does it all mean?

Even just taking the exit now becomes a process of calculated precision. In our mind, there can be no unfinished business, although we have some difficulty resolving what that business really is. Is it our partner, our children, or our community?

The value of community and partnership seem to come foremost in our minds, and in this part of our journey there is no doubt what lane we intend to take.

In that lane, the process of growth and refinement of the spirit goes on continually during our interaction with every person in a direct and meaningful way. Obviously, it is not the lane conducted and controlled by the machinery and its agents from the philosophy of opposites. Instead of organizing a community so that we can exploit it to the fullest for what we can get for our selfish desires, we mobilize communities to empower themselves to behave in a way that is for their own benefit.

It is ironic that we tend not to recognize the true benefits of a journey until we almost come to the end of it. Some of us barely indulge in the basic essentials at the rest stop so that we can hurry our way onto the exit with no contemplation on the purpose of our journey or the destination. Life's journey is a one way parkway and the experiences we acquire in the course of traveling are ratified through the enrichment of the spirit.

The wear and tear of the drudgeries of life in which we are engaged, and the tangibles or the material possessions are all subconscious efforts to help us attain our spiritual composure. How we use our rest stop is a clear indication of how we have lived our lives. Life's experiences have provided us with all the opportunities to extract the gems of wisdom they provided to enrich our spirit.

However, we can get so preoccupied with the sensational side shows that our lives become a series of quick stops to petty trinket stalls and roller coaster joy rides. We may have simply been too busy grasping at the illusions of cheap pleasures from the melodramas of political and social life that we ignored the magnetism that prevailed in the realms of our vision and understanding.

ATTRIBUTES OF THE SPIRIT

There is atmosphere that is seen and one that is unseen. The one that is unseen exists in as formidable a way as the one that is unseen, but can only be seen by the spirit in dimensions unknown to the naked eye. It speaks volumes to the mind that is awake and hungry for wisdom and upliftment.

When we learn to see through the spirit, the eye sees beyond the horizon, over hills, through walls and bodies, and windows of other eyes that are closed. There is much more to a relationship than what is physical and material, beyond the touch and the feel. It goes beyond the rudimentary indulgences of social and economic exchange, or even the emotional responses to need and circumstances. It is only when the mind can extend to the realm of the spiritual that it begins to unravel the mysteries of what connects us in the first place.

Much of what we do not recognize or that we take for granted may be the very essence of what our relationship is all about. However, we pretend to dismiss it or make it convenient for ourselves to ignore it. We think we can take the prerogative to dismiss something that is not tangible because there seems to be no basis to make ourselves accountable for it.

However, much of what we take for granted, we can hardly see or feel, forms the basis for our freedom. While elaborate systems generated from the philosophy of opposites struggle to engage us with the clamor of issues and attractions, it is the small and insignificant that proves to be most lethal and powerful. The very unassuming disposition attending to the ordinary attributes of life and love is what consumed us to the core, long before we recognize that it is even there. Like the innocence of a child, it makes no demands, declares no contest or offers no apologies for being what it is. It does not want to be, but is, and will always be.

INTERNAL AND EXTERNAL

The little things that we tend to miss, ignore, or even take for granted are the foundation on which our happiness is based. The extent of our happiness depends, however, on the level of freedom we have achieved in our lives, and in our relationship with ourselves and others. Any state or level of freedom begins from within. We must first be at peace with ourselves before peace can begin to prevail within.

The external interaction we facilitate in our interaction with others fosters the quality of interaction we encourage within ourselves. The world extends itself to us in ways that are unpredictable, sometimes problematic, but nearly always in ways that blend with our ideas and concepts from within. We may borrow or adopt an idea or concept we like, but it is natural for us to want to connect from within to factors and persons reaching to us from without.

It is natural for us to want to be at peace with our environment, beginning with our partner, our children and extending to everyone and everything else. We want to develop that harmony with the birds and the trees, and be able to hear the music they provide purely from their interaction. We are a part of that harmony and want to play our part in the song of life. That connection comes from the gifts of nature, and can only be made through the spirit. It needs no external gadgets of social class and political prestige, economic status, or ideological orientation. All of these latch down on our freedom, turning us into instruments and puppets of the unnatural world. They provide imitations that serve to distract us from our inner yearnings, and to bribe us with extensions so that we can adorn ourselves with the glittering jewels of self-aggrandizement. We become burdened with rituals and routines that turn us away from our true selves and we get preoccupied with the endless clamor of melodramatics orchestrated by the machinery of society.

Jerry S. Barry

FREEDOM AND THE ACT OF WILL

Freedom is an act of the spirit, a determination of the mind over matter that is stronger than any force of physical power.

It is more internal than external, for it is an intrinsic reflection of our philosophy of life and our relationships with others. As benevolent as our intentions may be, we can hardly free someone from the malignancies of their lives.

They must first recognize and then acknowledge their condition, even as we lay hands on the dragnet that imprisons them. We can help to loosen the knots that they may not be able to reach, but it is only the victim who can know his or her true restrictions; therefore only the victim can truly detach the fetters to make himself or herself free. It is an act of will that is stronger than bullets or swords, arrows or cannonballs, chains or legal restrictions that are enforced by impoverished minds. It is this act of will that brings us back to the center of our true selves, balancing us with nature and the true purpose of our existence. It is the force that fuels our obligations to our partner, to our offspring and all with whom we come into contact, bringing us to the equilibrium that is essential to our lives. Force is a phenomenon that is hardly ever seen or heard, but is most definitely felt with full strength once it lands at the point of impact. Will is also never seen and also never heard, except from the weak resolve of braggarts and mendicants who want to be seen or heard for their hollow theories and shallow intentions. The act of will is truly the expression of the spirit.

The act of will gives us the final resolve to take the ramp for the exit into Winter. This is the phase when we need to prepare ourselves because we are nearing the point of realizing the purpose of our life's journey. Our first exit out of Spring had been full of the shades of discovery in our travel. It seemed that it wasn't until after our trip that we began to learn, but that depended on our level of consciousness.

We can live this life savoring every moment for what it is worth only if our insights are not flavored by expectations from the predigested thinking of grand illusions. If only our spirit could be left alone, uninterrupted and undisturbed, to discover naturally the wisdom of the moment, the pleasures of being in the present, synchronizing during transition the moment that is ours, then every step of the journey will have been well spent. When the discovery in Spring graduates into the excitement in Summer, then the gift of light and warmth brings new discoveries of their own.

Each season brings its own joys and challenges into the revolving cycles of life as we grow and evolve into our true selves. Then we are able to pollinate the flowers of opportunity that enrich the world around us with the decisions we make. Each phase is a cycle of enrichment that redefines our perspective for the journey that we take. The gift of each season brings its joys, but only when we savor it for what it offers us. Only then can we truly acquire the benefits of our original aspirations.

Life has its mysteries strewn along its highway

Life has its mysteries strewn along its highway, glittering like jewels on the markers of the lanes that we travel. Those jewels that we do not grasp in the present become history to glitter in the chalice of our regrets. That is only if we recognize them, or time will consume them into the darkness of our past. Regrets can bring with them their wisdom, like jewels in the raw, waiting to be polished. Each day brings its own shower of blessings, some which we can capture in the moment and others we can appreciate falling like raindrops along the way.

The secret is to relish the portion that is ours within our realm of understanding and saturate our spirit with their benefits like a lotion to our soul. If we can arrive at that level of consciousness, then preparing to exit into winter becomes more a matter of compulsion than a mere ritual. We need to prepare ourselves for the external but certainly not for the internal.

The spirit is forever alert and ready to grasp its daily portion of wisdom from the passing experiences of life.

A mind that is preoccupied with the glamour of parades and superficial issues will hardly connect with the joys of the spirit because it will miss the jewels of wisdom along the way. Like fastening our seatbelts for the journey, we need to properly connect to the spiritual aspects of life, so that all other things can fall into place. It seems that this

175

time we have to be more decisive in how we prepare on this part of our journey since the ramp is hardly visible in the darkness and bleak fog, and the very surface of which we travel presents a challenge from ice and snow.

However, the highway beyond the ramp appears less crowded than usual. Most travelers seem to be making the most of the rest stop here in reluctance to engage with the weather conditions ahead of them. Just looking ahead at the atmosphere it is easy to conclude that we would have to make adjustments in order to proceed with our journey. Our adjustments depend on our needs and shortcomings.

For some of us, it is easier to go into denial, perhaps by putting on the performance of a lifetime to bring attention to things that are irrelevant. The more flamboyant the props and settings, the more convincing the melodrama can be; but the longer and harder we perform on this stage, the more difficult it is to approach the ramp for our winter journey.

The mystery that lurks within this phase of our travel creeps steadily into our minds, making the journey seem very precarious even before we begin. It is perhaps the first time we feel compelled to consider the purpose of our journey and the nature of our destination. We have already completed three phases of our journey, and the experiences gained through them should have trained us to be alert enough to scan with utmost efficiency for the gems of wisdom every moment can provide. If we had been making our journey fully induced in the spirit, we should be able to make the ramp with our eyes closed.

Jerry S. Barry

**Winter is no different a journey than that of Autumn,
Summer, or Spring.**

WINTER

Now that we have merged onto the highway and
into the winter of our lives, the mist that made this
season seem so bleak in the distance begins to clear
into scenes our eyes can now behold. Before long,
we come to realize what a great privilege it is to
have come this far, and that this phase of our
journey is the most crucial to the fulfillment of our
aspirations. Before we took the exit ramp, the
world behind the fog ahead of us was shrouded in

the mystery of a silent, cold mystique and the raw solitude of a desert.

In many ways, the atmosphere of winter is very similar to that of a desert. The extremes in temperatures of each can create the illusion that the places and circumstances within these environments are exclusively different as they deny the common denominators within that conform to the normal cycles or patterns around which life revolves. If we can ignore the strange environments but observe the patterns within them, we will discover that the sequences of events and circumstances in each season is one and the same.

Winter is no different a journey than that of Autumn, Summer, or Spring. It is the dynamics that occupy our minds within the season, the priorities that engage us and the meanings we adopt in the course of travel that set the tone of the season's outcome. The phase of uncertainty from which we came slowly unwinds itself into certainty, from the depth of darkness that eventually leads to the light.

Our journey's direction is only one-way, but what we have taken with us are the gems of understanding and the ideas to build our stature and awareness to prepare for the next challenge. The nature of these events and circumstances is the same as any other season, except that we risk getting caught up in expectations that are based on the illusions that we may allow to cloud our vision.

Every season and every stage within them brings its own illusions that can distort and surprise. The aura surrounding them can be like that of a shopping mall, which is designed to make us feel like honored guests in a heavenly place, the land of luxury, abundance, and bliss. We may come to realize, if we are lucky to awaken to our real senses by then, that every detail of what we see and hear, has been meticulously orchestrated and choreographed to help us to interpret, understand, and deal with the void that has formed in our minds. Usually, it is this void that has brought us to the mall, and that is what keeps us there perpetually seeking ways and means to satisfy our unnatural appetite.

In our Spring, there was a natural tendency to want to be pampered and cared for, when we had barely begun to understand our mission or purposes in life. Then, our knowledge and expectations about the world had been based on the providence of our parents, our culture, and the institutions of our society. We excused ourselves for our shortcomings, for wanting to be pampered into a state of helplessness, building within our minds expectations that were unreal, if not ridiculous.

WINTER ILLUSIONS

When we exist within an environment of illusions that extends beyond the reality of our true nature, we will aspire to those amenities that blur our vision to the extent that we will live in a state of fantasy. Fantasy is good in the beginning, as it is a perfect recipe for the dreams and aspirations that will fuel our pursuits later in life. This childish tendency never really leaves us, but simply transforms with age as we journey down the highways and byways of life.

As adults, we still carry the germ of the child within us yearning to be pampered and to be excused for our misgiving. It reveals itself in Summer in our reckless abandon for pleasure seeking and all manners of dangerous intrigues in the name of youth, as we compile the mistakes we have made to give ourselves good reasons to boast of our regrets.

A life journey that is dominated by illusions is lived like a car skidding on its wheels even when the roads are dry and the sun is shining. Such lives are preoccupied with all manners of restrictions and limitations that sacrifice the present potential of bliss for anxieties and fears of the future, which are linked to demons of the past.

When our perception is blurred by the predicament of a disillusioned mind, life takes us for a ride down paths full of circumstances and events that are beyond our control. We can hardly afford to surrender ourselves to compromises when our traction on the road in winter is crucial, not only for our safety and enrichment, but also our sanity and peace of mind. If we are not squarely grounded in our true nature, and have been disoriented and misguided, winter can become a journey on a roadway paved with speculation and anxiety.

As our options become narrower due to the way we think, the road narrows too. We focus on every pebble or hump upon the road and all the imperfections of the surface, but keeping our eyes firmly fixed on the road in fear of what we may see is not the best way to make a journey. When we focus on the mundane details of life's circumstances and the petty material obstructions and rewards, we miss the bigger spiritual benefits of life's bounty and the daily downpours of gifts of every kind that are assigned to our better selves.

Beyond the ramp, the fog and the mist, there is a haven that welcomes us despite our pitfalls of doubt and regret. When we are able to release ourselves from the limitations of our past, what we behold ceases to be an illusion, and our eyes are relieved from trying to make sense of a worn and bumpy road.

Illusions can seem very real depending upon the viewer's state of mind. They can be formed externally when the fog is caught in an incidental refraction of light, projecting images and forms with much conviction and accuracy. Our first impulse is to attach some meaning to what meets the eye, but these meanings are still only determined by the connections we can make to what we see based on our experiences.

Beyond the ramp, the fog and the mist, there is a haven that welcomes us

That is why our first reaction can be one of panic, pain or displeasure if our related experience had been negative, or it can be one of excitement if our experience had been positive.

Therefore, the impact of the external is determined or influenced by the internal. What our mind chooses to perceive is what our eye is most likely to see. What resides within our internal spiritual world is more likely to shape the experiences we have in our external world. The lane before us narrows when we think in terms of our limitations, and it widens when we think in terms of our capabilities. It is not necessarily what we see or what is there, but instead how prepared and alert our mind is to make the most of unique opportunities that come our way. Each season brings its own tidal wave of opportunities, and winter is no exception. Such tides encounter us at intersections in formal or informal ways. We may miss the tide when we are not ready or alert enough, or even when we simply fail to recognize it.

MISINTERPRETATIONS

---

*Much of what we identify as trials
and tribulations may very well be
misrepresented opportunities,
because we were not ready or failed
to recognize it as such.*

It may very well be also that when we are not looking down, we are looking back through seasons and experiences that have passed, and not being willing to acknowledge that the context had changed. The richness of a season can only be extracted within the context of that season and no other, although one season may help to prepare us for the coming of the next.

Perhaps the biggest challenge we face in life is learning not only to recognize, but also learning how to tap into the showers of blessings that come with each season, and then what to do with the virtual treasures we have extracted. If we happen to miss out on one season, it is crucial for us to learn how and why we did, so that we can develop the skills and insight to garnish the virtues of the other seasons that follow.

Winter should, therefore, not be viewed as the culmination of all the seasons, but as a season unto itself; separated and yet connected. We can enjoy Winter just as much as we enjoy Autumn, Summer and Spring. We should not waste the virtues of Winter by celebrating the virtues and accomplishments of another season. A life of regret is the result of a whole journey of lost or wasted opportunities, not because the opportunities were not there, but because we did not recognize them or use them to our benefit.

Life is about changing and evolving,
not fossilizing and confining
ourselves within the vacuums of past
comforts, victories and
disappointments.

Even the present moment in which we exist is moving and traveling in the continuous tense, and with every second that we freeze and hesitate we render ourselves out of context and out of place. Our philosophy and internal reasoning must be able to aid us in hovering around or absorbing the shocks of the potholes so that life can remain a cruise.

THE PECULIAR AND THE RUDIMENTARY

When we focus on the rudimentary, we are looking down at the potholes and bumps to pick and accumulate material benefits, social aggrandizements, and fame. We ensnare ourselves with these obstructions to our real nature instead of looking up at the gifts of the spirit showering on us at every turn. When our minds are obsessed with the mundane and material, we tend not to know when to turn up our umbrellas to enjoy the downpour. When we allow ourselves to get trapped within the philosophy of opposites, we lock ourselves into a vacuum that is contradictory to our true nature, and abandon ourselves to the cheap pleasures of the immediate and the ordinary. Without realizing it, we are at a standstill, grabbing and juggling illusions, bubbles of empty enjoyments that distract from the real opportunities to enrich the spirit. What makes our journey worthwhile is the opportunity and privilege to pursue the things that matter to the fulfillment of our true nature according to the dictates of our spirit. That is not accomplished from dictates outside of us but from deep burning aspirations from within us.

It is not so much the living, but rather the quality of life we have lived. It is not so much the journey, but what we have done along the way, and how we have polished the moments of time into jewels and enriched this world with the imprints of our steps. The things that matter have nothing to do with material things or the triviality of social status and fame. The things that matter are more concerned with embracing the dictates of the spirit, and connecting with the network of universal intelligence for the upliftment of humanity.

When we become preoccupied with the material, we need more and more of it to assure ourselves and others that we are comfortable and fulfilled. Yet, with an appetite that knows no bounds, we relentlessly pursue more with unlimited indiscretion. We proceed further to build physical and social walls around us to preserve and protect our gains from those who have little or nothing.

Our idea of evolving revolves around getting more and building more containers and enclosures to secure our possessions and ourselves. Everybody else, including our loved ones, revolves around this vicious cycle of getting, expanding, and preserving. The spirit, however, needs no physical conduit to assure itself, be it money, property, or fame. Its values and pursuits are on a different plane. Its territory and aspirations are unlimited, expanding beyond boundaries into the realm of dreams. Like its archenemies, it knows no limit, not because it has to strive to achieve, but because it is limitless in nature.

Those of us who are under the influence of the spirit do not feel the need to look around for approval, or to follow meticulous rituals to prove ourselves and their mission. We simply wait for the bounties of the spirit to shower on us.

The mysteries of life are no mystery to the spirit. As we make our journey through the perplexities of life, it is the subconscious that helps us to see without looking, steer without turning, and brake without crashing. As we get more seasoned in our travels, our subconscious is meant to take over when our spirit goes into overdrive to take us over the hills to higher grounds of thought. Reality then becomes the preference of the internal, not the ritual indulgence with the routine and the external.

Material comforts and their social aggrandizement are of little concern to the spirit. For those of us who are still stuck on the material, still focused on priorities that are controversial to our true nature, the road narrows as we progressively operate on the basis of our limitations. That is when we continue to think in terms of rest stops and banquets, pageants and ceremonies with indulgences in superfluous excesses for its own sake.

THE EGO AND THE SPIRIT

The ego has an appetite that knows no bounds. It can grow to a colossal obstruction beyond our control, consuming our energies with peripheral pursuits that are mere obsessions and addictions. Our wheels may be rolling on the surface of the road, but real driving involves looking ahead to the horizon at the wider prospects of travel.

A mind that is free will be able to take to the hill to observe the other horizons beyond it. When we move by the dictates of the spirit, our horizon unfolds with new layers of truth as the whole nature of our journey changes.

The spirit has its own conclusions and solutions that are as concrete and absolute as nature itself. The journey of life is like a business, and the business of life is also governed by a goal or mission. Any business that abandons or neglects its mission becomes a boat with a broken rudder, stumbling over its decisions and always drifting towards a rocky shore. The internal preferences of the spirit take us to the next level of enlightenment as we begin to recognize new dimensions of our aspirations. In our physical, natural world we may seem to be the same, performing the same routines of our job or profession and using our bodies in apparently normal ways.

However, as the spirit unfolds our sense of purpose and our true enlightenment, we begin to experience outbursts of pleasure that have little or nothing to do with what we had done before. That is when the physical becomes the means to the spiritual ends. That is when we begin our journey from the physical and the external to the internal or spiritual. We have entered into a phase of dual existence, where our actions and intentions are likely to be misunderstood by everyone around us. Our interactions with our loved ones and others can gradually become punctuated with disappointments and surprises.

They still see us in the physical and judge our actions and existence according to their expectations. They are still relating to us from the platform of life where they exist, judging our actions through their fears and desires, and connecting to us for the fulfillment of material and social benefits. We would like to be able to interpret our transition in ways for them to understand, but they continue to hold on to the ghosts of our former selves because it suits the priorities of their present world. Gradually, as we get closer to the horizon, a new kind of reality appears, and we find ourselves alone. We become the journey and the journey becomes a part of us.

Jerry S. Barry

The mission we have in life is never meant to center around us individually, as it transcends and envelops the network of humanity. The needs and aspirations of others are channeled through us in ways that are unusual and often unpredictable. For those of us who travel within the realms of the spirit, no situation that demands our service and attention is problematic.

Life itself is an investment in the cycle that operates the universe, and this network depends on us to keep to our paths. When we abandon our obligations, we banish ourselves to be suspended in a periphery of darkness, forever grappling among ourselves for material satisfaction in the world of tangibles. The mission of life is continuously being renewed and revived as the network draws from the source of supreme intelligence.

Those who are connected in the spirit are also connected to fulfillment and enlightenment, becoming sources of light and enlightenment themselves.

We are alone, not because the obligations and focus to our mission is unique and self-fulfilling. When we invest ourselves into our mission, we can transform the material into magical in ways that stun the ordinary mind. The ordinary is forever being fashioned into the extraordinary once it has entered the process of our thoughts and actions. When we invest ourselves in the mission of the spirit, there are no boundaries of time, ethnicity, nationality, religion or geographic location. We become part of a network of energy that is limitless and boundless. We are no longer in phases of experimentation and discovery as when we were in Spring, Summer and Autumn.

LIVING IN THE SPIRIT

There is, or ought to be, confidence and assurance of spirit in those that have reached the Winter of their lives. They are not interested in gloating over accomplishments of the past, or the material accumulations of the present. The fears and uncertainties of the future are of little concern to them. When we are fully invested in the mission of our lives, we fuse together the past, the present and the future by the very way we think, act, or speak.

Those who are invested with the intuitions of the spirit understand the significance of time in ways that combine all its virtues and energy to create new dimensions of reality that is useful to mankind. There is no dead past, impotent present or uncertain future. They are all distorted figments of our vision and ways of thinking that has been installed from the philosophy of opposites. We are part of history and history is a part of us. The present is under our control in all the ways we are able to contrive through our imagination. We are therefore, the vehicle through which the future waits to flourish. When we get fixated in the past, allowing ourselves to be controlled and dominated by it, we are misusing a valuable instrument that can define our present to eventually dictate our future.

By failing to interpret life's experiences as vital lessons for growth and enrichment, we burrow ourselves in fear of the present and become virtual fossils in the sands of time, leaving a future unattended and awaiting the contribution only we can give. To refer to history in a peripheral, disconnected manner is equivalent to letting someone else interpret its events and circumstances for us. In both instances we are not counted, only being used conveniently to support or aggrandize someone else.

When we learn to interpret history for our own benefit, we can recognize ourselves in the presence of our ancestors in ways that are personal and eclectic. We can be present in the lives of those that went before us in ways only we can determine. We can also stand aside as spectators and theorize about possibilities and conclusions to make ourselves feel energized with golden memories of the past.

The choices we make about how we want to interact with our past will determine the mold that will shape our future. What is unique about traveling in Winter is the lack of visibility, as the moisture within the atmosphere weighs heavily with other surrounding circumstances within the location. However, in life, as in any journey, everything is relative, and conditions will continue to vary and even contradict as we move along.

Nature will continue to be what it has always been: true to itself regardless of who or what traverses its path. It does not alter its function or mission according to the whims or needs of any traveler. It simply is, has been, and will always be itself in whatever it does. We are the travelers, Nature is not. We sample the benefits of its gifts as we go along. It does not differentiate or discriminate in how it dispenses its qualities or performs its functions. Our interaction with nature is very relative to where we are and how we see ourselves in relation to the natural course of events around us. We cannot change the weather around us, but we can certainly determine the impact it has on us by the manner in which we relate to it. It is futile to complain or even wish for conditions that are different. That is the common indulgence of a feeble mind and a misguided, self-indulgent spirit.

When the fog and the mist gather,
and visibility is almost
impossible, it is the spirit that
becomes our autopilot to
transition us into the new
possibilities of our lives.

**Winter is perhaps the worst season in life to run and crash
into an obstacle**

HAZARDS OF WINTER TRAVEL

This is why it is so important to keep our spirit pure and uncontaminated by the negativity exuded by the insipid philosophy of opposites. There are diseases of the mind that lure the spirit onto a path of false expectations and distorts our vision during those crucial moments when we need to be most alert on the road.

False expectations can also disguise themselves in enticing costumes of glamour and material rewards that can tempt us into driving off course into a ravine or a ditch. For those of us who are gullible for great expectations of riches and fame, this may be the cliff that can derail our lives altogether. That is when it can become convenient to project the blame for our situation away from ourselves. It is easier to make an excuse that the bad weather conditions made it hard to see, or that some other traveler cut into our path and forced us into making an alternative decision.

Winter is perhaps the worst season in life to run and crash into an obstacle. At a period when we should be exploring the many new possibilities unfolding, we should not have to be picking up scattered pieces of ourselves. A crisis or tragedy that builds around the circumstances in our lives is more likely to be the result of many smaller mishaps that have accumulated repeatedly over a long period of time due to a lack of attention on our part. By repeating smaller mistakes, we give them the potential to become bigger and more difficult to correct, which makes us less competent to deal with them. If we had been paying attention, we would have noticed the little bumps on the road and adjusted our driving to accommodate the shocks and minor inconsistencies.

All the big crises in our lives tend to start with small, petty, and seemingly irrelevant incidents that we choose to dismiss as inconsequential. We do not realize that, contained in those petty details, are opportunities to prepare ourselves for bigger life challenges ahead when our stature and internal consciousness gradually increase with time.

What starts out as a simple oversight can become a major obstacle to our internal peace and comfort. Any issue that threatens to or actually derails us emotionally is an issue of the spirit.

Anything, whether it is an event, person or circumstance that penetrates our being to the inside, finds its target in the weakness or deficiency of the spirit within us. The spirit itself is never really distracted from its mission and sense of purpose. It may, however, be interrupted and shift into parking mode until we are finished with peripheral issues. The spirit never gets involved with petty material issues that are the obsessions of small minds. Distracting ourselves with petty infractions is like putting on a blindfold while taking an important turn on the highway.

When we are at peace with our spirit, our viewpoint is as clear as an open landscape, and the median that balances our outlook and reasoning is ever present to guide us day or night. Distractions have always paraded along the highway even in Spring, Summer and Autumn, accosting us with neon lights of sudden urges and desires.

As veterans on the highways of life, we should have previously developed the tolerance to any efforts to lure us away from our true path. We should already know that these offers of success, fame and immediate satisfaction are actually demons in disguise from the philosophy of opposites. Even in Winter, they are camouflaged among the ice and snow, and invite us to their excursions in the breakdown lane. They may even create false exits for us to change our course in the hopes that we will develop new toxic aspirations.

MISSIONS, PURPOSES AND ENTRAPMENTS

The purpose of a journey is not decided in the course of that journey, and lasting aspirations are initiated from within, where the spirit abides, and not from without where passing phases of growth and consciousness can create mirages of grandeur for which the heart may mistakenly aspire. The heart can create realms of material and social fulfillment that can be contradictory to the spirit, for it is not the heart but the spirit that holds the key to the mission of our lives. The heart is quick to sympathize and empathize on issues. That is when the slipping and sliding begins, and we can begin to swerve and make impromptu turns out of pure speculation.

The dreams and speculations of the heart almost never synchronize with those of the spirit, but they can be equally as convincing to the human mind. The heart can even try to overwhelm the spirit with a flood of good intentions that have little or nothing to do with the mission of our lives.

It is during Winter, when the need for warmth and companionship becomes intense, that this conflict of interest becomes paramount and problematic. The heart may be inclined to interpret and respond to circumstances in ways that can exploit the good intentions of the spirit. There are people and events that can prey on the good will contained in the mission of our lives, bending it conveniently with pretentious and submissive acts of coercion that can melt even the sternest heart. They can entrap us in a web of self-pity or of self-sacrificing goodness that seems to blend with the mission of our spirit to the extent where we may accept them as part of our mission.

Our mission of goodwill can be usurped by crafty predators who position themselves to enjoy our good graces in order to satisfy their own selfish egotistic ambitions. We must be very cautious of hitchhikers that can attach like parasites to profit from our gains. We need to be most alert for the ones who put on an act of being desperately stranded and even disguise themselves to look genuine.

The hazards of traveling can come more from the travelers involved rather than just the road or the weather. The worst among them are those wandering around looking for something exciting to do at the expense of someone else. They have no clear mission, or any constructive interpretation of time or space. These are the plagiarists, the parasites and the predators who seek to hitch on to our accomplishments for a free ride in life.

Their only ambition is to make plagiarists of us too, the authors of our own success. Such people are on the constant lookout for successful people, to establish some contact and to be associated with them. They may have become preoccupied with rumors about successful people and invested themselves in reshaping and circulating drippings of news into rumors just for their own entertainment.

Like true agents from the system of opposites, they prefer to lay in wait in the periphery of the accomplishments of others, and engineer spinoffs to give themselves a presence associated with great things and important people. Out of these tangents of the truth they dwell upon the speculation and the sensation to direct attention to themselves as the persons of substance, grace, and wisdom. Take careful note of all the seriously ambitious and dedicated achievers who have to deal with these human leeches hovering around them like flies, doing little more than contaminating the space of the persons they have targeted.

What makes it most unfortunate is that these vermin may even be counted among our loved ones, or friends and associates who had worked to win our trust and confidence. They lunge with precision when visibility is poor, and when our options in life seem to have narrowed. They show up to offer sympathy when in fact they are getting ready to strike when we are most vulnerable, and at the turning points in our lives.

ENEMIES IN THE JOURNEY OF LIFE

Our worst enemies can be those who are closest to us, sharing our dreams and comforts in a world of which they do not belong. Those who have no dreams of their own wear a mask so that they can become part of ours, although it does not reduce the anguished feelings of envy, jealousy, and hate associated with their empty spirit. They tolerate the dedication we give to our mission, which is adverse to theirs, waiting patiently for the tide to turn on us so that they can reap the spoils when we fall.

It is, however, ironic that our encounters with travelers of this kind are all part of the course of the journey that we take, and that they are nevertheless essential for our spiritual growth and refinement. We do not suffer disappointment when weaklings celebrate their victory over the material crumbs they manage to obtain at our expense. We are neither interested in the things they gloat upon, nor do we want to be associated with the cheap victories of underlings. They are obsessed with the material and are on a different plane of existence and consciousness, and can hardly comprehend the reasons for things happening in their own lives much less ours. They are so engrossed in their yearnings and desires for the immediate pleasures of life, that they can hardly see or feel beyond what is before them. Like a delinquent child consuming a piece of candy he or she has stolen, they are too occupied with the taste in their mouths to project their minds towards the consequences of their actions.

Why, therefore, should we interrupt the fulfillment of our own redemption to dwell on the actions and intentions of persons sworn to a false, petty mission in their lives? Why then, would we contaminate ourselves in getting peeved and fretting over their wrong actions and decisions because of the bond, blood, or social connection that we share with them? Should we let our loyalty be extended that far to jeopardize our own spiritual enrichment for their sake?

That will be exactly what we do when we compromise and try to use our powers of persuasion. People who exist solely in material realm will hardly be persuaded to give up their pleasures and addictions to fulfill their obligations to even the ones they love. There can be no true love with the feebleminded; there will always be layers of pretexts and excuses to apologize for mishaps and mistakes, truces to be made for lines that have been crossed, and principles that have been violated that have to be revised again and again. To travel with people such as those in any season, no amount of spare tires would be enough.

Persons with mediocre intentions will always burn our tires to the rim because of the heat that will develop from their philosophy of opposites. There will be the heaviness of greed and discontent and the deadweight of a stubborn soul that refuses to compromise even to coexist for basic survival. They will have an allegiance to others of their kind to help sabotage our mission, and afterward, only to return to their various schemes of obstruction. The determination of the weak and indulgent only serves to further strengthen the resolve of those guided by the spirit.

We can afford to empathize with their turmoil and distress and even accommodate their shortcomings because we are not hooked by shallow aspirations. It is not necessary for us to control or subdue them to maintain our peace of mind. There is a defensive kind of understanding that keeps our world separate from theirs. This separation prevents the annoyance that would probably cause accidents for us.

How wonderful it would be if we could share the same outlook, aspirations and dreams for the enjoyments of this life. It would seem logical that we would be better off in our travels without the interjections of shadow demons in human form who are bent on one single mission and that is to distract, discourage or destroy us in the course of travel. That is what the agents from the philosophy of opposites would like to think they are doing to us when they resist our way of life. Since they think that way, they are easily satisfied with what they are doing, assuming that their action is having adverse effects on our actions and decisions.

THE POSITIVE EFFECT OF THE NEGATIVE

Our travels during the winter season would be so mundane, routine, and even stagnant if we did not have the challenges from these adversaries to help light up our path. It is the power and determination of our adversary that establishes the dynamics of our spiritual pursuits. We do not resist or struggle with them personally but against the principles on which they operate.

That is why we can always see them without looking, hear them without listening, and resist their greatest efforts without raising a hand. It is the darkness of their intentions that becomes the electricity for our efforts, and it is their persistence that makes us calm. It is through them that we are able to assure ourselves of who or what we would not like to be. It is perhaps more true than we can ever imagine that opposites attract. We are not attracted to our adversaries because we need them, or any of their materialistic qualities. We are attracted because, in comparison to their contrasting qualities, we can reassure ourselves that we are on the right track in our pursuits.

We do not and will not ever want to be like them because they are not free. They are not free because they cannot be themselves and have no control over their own identities. When what you are is inextricably linked to what you want and what you have, then you inevitably become what you have or want to have. These people are powerless and insipid without their fancy clothes and adornments, social prestige and connections, material possessions and fame that are all associated with the philosophy of opposites.

What they do not realize is that those frivolities have attached them to a giant machinery that controls their whole being; how they walk, talk, create meanings, and even think. They become part of a herd driven by a circle of desires and addictions designed by a network that does not even value their existence. Their network wants to guarantee their contribution to a wider culture of falsities and self-esteem based on degenerate standards of behavior. Their enjoyments of life are linked to neon lights, plenty of noise and clamor, and parades of necromancy and social intrigue.

They are blind to the evil predicament in which their lives are suspended because they are too caught up in the whirlpool of its power grid. They are like a child excited by the thrill of a roller coaster ride. They become so obsessed with the thrill of the moment that they ignore the implications and the circumstances involved until it is too late. Perhaps it would be more appropriate to say that they dismissed rather than ignored these implications when we take into account the orientations that they give themselves. Perhaps it is even more difficult to conceive that persons like ourselves who have travelled this far into the journey of our lives would project such a shallow outlook on the richness of this life.

That is probably why they are so irresistibly attracted to people invested in the spirit. It could be that they somehow suspect that, while they hoard material riches in their pockets, people invested in the spirit seem to have riches overflowing in their hearts. It is by the same creed of greed and envy by which they are fatally attracted to people with higher ideals. It is their secret yearning to escape darkness to experience a portion of our light, even if it means to steal it from us.

It is so hard for them to comprehend that the light of the spirit is not something we can give to them; it is a quality they have to take for themselves. It is a choice or option they can attach to their lives to elevate to the next plain of their existence. They can hardly appreciate how that existence is even possible while they are surrounded by the darkness of their own intentions, binding themselves in chains of exotic tastes and desires, and limiting themselves behind the bars of limitation they have adopted. Even when they strive to graduate to higher intentions to aspire to the light, they attempt to steal it from us. That is because they are still stuck with the notion of equating the spiritual with the material. That is when they get lost again in the perpetual cycle of reversals, between the neon lights of their dark world and a glimpse of heavenly truth. They want to compare the light of the spirit with the glitter of the gold in their hands.

Nevertheless, it is their inclination towards the darkness that reveals to them our light. It is their attachment to the material that weighs them down heavily to their base intentions in everything they say and do. It is our light that they seek. The level of freedom that we enjoy is what they are aspiring to accomplish. They are so controlled by events and circumstances, they live in constant fear of being consumed. With the reserves that they have compiled over the years, they still want to hitch a ride from us to be within reach of what they think we have. Even the best of their intentions are plagued with illusions.

THE PHILOSOPHY OF OPPOSITES IN WINTER

By placing all their confidence in things that are material, they have resigned themselves into the depth of darkness, into the bottomless pit of hopelessness and discontent. In that world, they can never have enough because all things material are constantly dissolving or disintegrating into dust. Even the value of currency is unstable and fluctuates by demand and supply. To place our confidence in material things that are linked to a value system is similar to comparing our emotions and feelings of self-worth to the fluctuations of money markets and equivalent systems.

The philosophy of opposites conditions their consciousness to that kind of culture of the material power grid where certainty and uncertainty can be reversible within the same time frame like lights blinking on and off in a disco club to get us in the mood for dancing. It is a strategy to keep people suspended between two opposite emotions at the same time so that they are unable to analyze either of them. It helps that person to develop a bipolar tendency of flipping conveniently from one state of consciousness to the other.

The philosophy of opposites conditions them to aspire to be proud victims of circumstance, using their deficiencies as a prerogative to demand the commitment and loyalty of others. Their warmth is so infested with intrigue, that the atmosphere around them is loaded with negativity and harmful radiation. Even in the best of their intentions, they can more explain what is wrong than look for a way or even attempt to fix it right.

Even in Winter, our pathways are charged with encounters that challenge our sophistication, reminding us that to whom much is given, much is expected. It is usually true also that those who put us high up on the pedestals of their expectations do not match them with their obligations. They want to hold us ransom on the standards they expect from us, but they give themselves the prerogatives to prey upon our virtues. While we empathize with them and the predicament of their circumstances, we must be careful not to get caught up in their traffic.

We do not belong in the lane of the materialistic where hypocrites and predators prevail under all manner of false pretenses and disguises. In Winter we should avoid the breakdown lane where associates, acquaintances, relatives and friends abound. Their persuasions are slippery and may bring us too close to the edge of a ravine, where predators await a generous feast on account of some good person's misfortune.

Some predators operate by night where conditions would favor their dark intentions. Some lay waiting in the breakdown lane where they can tap into the first hint of insecurity that could give us a flat. Then there are the critters with virtually no polish or grace in their outlook, or clandestine operations that lurk in the deep woods of complicated societal affairs. There are shrubs in politics and business that would promptly entangle us, while concealing or even protecting those that rightfully belong there.

Murky swamps that are almost impossible to negotiate but are as attractive as a coral seabed are the favorite domains of the slippery kinds, who manipulate their destinies of others for their benefit and satisfaction on the premise of promises and hope.

Some predators operate by night

RETRIBUTION: LIFE PRODUCES IT LIKE A WORK OF ART

It is not a good driving habit to keep your eyes focused on every little detail that litters the highway, except when it is a thread to your vehicle or impedes your ability to travel.

If we must look, we must do so with a purpose, the least of which is to posthumously condemn the drivers you do not know or why and how they made their mistakes. Rather, we should resolve to empathize always with those victims of any accident in ways that empowers us to foresee possibilities of such occurrences in our own journey and in our lives. Being careful and alert is not sufficient to help us avoid an accident. An accident is a relative occurrence between two or more factors or two persons surprised blinded or distracted by the actions or intentions of each other. The accident or collusion is the result of a process in which all parties involved had participated in one way or the other.

Mistakes occur within the context of the current permeating circumstances that may prove very difficult to decipher subsequently. Those are the circumstance we should try to recreate so that we can envisage all the possibilities from them to protect ourselves from repeating those mistakes in our own driving. In this way, all drivers are brothers and sisters bonded together by the mitigation or possibilities of circumstances that occur during travel. Another driver's mishap is our warning of what could happen to us. No one is invincible, invulnerable or infallible when driving on the road, and the highway of life gives us numerous opportunities for us to explore that fact. By forgiving your brother, you accept his fault as your own and feel his pain to redeem yourself from repeating his mistake.

An attitude of sympathetic understanding and forgiveness gets the windscreen wipers going to clear the fog and debris in the eyes of our mind. We see better where we learn how to understand the limitations of others or to find ways to help them.

Those of us who cannot or will not forgive have our own reasons for doing so. It could be that we ourselves are debris makers and have made victims of many people along the way. The debris remind us of ourselves and what we have done to others, and will probably continue to do until we get a startling arousal from complacency. It can be childish fun and mischievousness to create debris in the life of others, especially when even as an adult, we see no reason to be penitent about it. That is why, in the ecstasy of our ignorance, we are forced to look, and to focus on misdeeds in the debris of life to feed the lust in our sick hearts for the things that we ourselves have done. That is why, even as we look, we become equally guilty and afraid, because we realize that someone is ahead of us and might have left these debris behind. There is reason to fear that we could be the victim of that evil person and that the next set of debris could be ours. So, we tighten our grip on the steering wheel and stiffen our body to high alert to save ourselves from someone just like us. A paranoid driver is intoxicated by his own fears and may do worse on the highway than someone physically intoxicated with drugs or alcohol. He may focus so intently and never see. He begins to hallucinate when he imagines his own intentions being carried out by other people who create debris in his life. He focuses on his guilt and his imagination and does not realize that he has already crossed his lane. When we are guilty of what we did in our past, we always become inhibited and tense when we drive. Hallucinations occur and we fail to take control of ourselves and make both debris and victim of ourselves. On the highways of life, the law of retribution follows the layout of the sketch that we make in life, then completes the picture like a work of art for us to behold in shock and total denial.

Jerry S. Barry

THE WINTER REST STOP

There is not much incentive to take a rest stop at this phase. There is little to nothing to see on the outside except for the performances of nature. Those travelers who would otherwise warm the atmosphere with their personalities are now tucked away into secure enclosures of their own, into spaces defined by their needs or limitations. This is when it is harder to analyze faces and to share glimpses of truth. Everyone seems stowed away inside the cocoon of what they would like others to see.

Most travelers still have their hoods on, bringing with them the security of their coats as if to pretend that they are not outside. They walk and look past each other as if preoccupied with their own missions. It is possible, though, that they are pretending to be cold and passive, when actually they yearn for the warmth of friendship and companionship, and a little exchange of genuine warmth to change the temperature of their lives.

Winter is prone to attracting the culture of weakness, a resignation of one's fate to persons and circumstances to the point of total surrender. Like an epidemic, there hangs in the air the belief that events are predetermined and that our self-will has lost its strength and potency, and that we are at the mercy of some unknown prophecy. When the mind reads it and the body accepts it, the outcome is sealed before we even know what that prophecy is.

Thus begins the reshaping of our lives, as we adjust our vision to a different perspective on life, convincing ourselves about things we have just come to believe. The atmosphere of Winter can bring its own persuasions for the weary traveler who has lost his or her way within.

When belief surmounts our conviction, and we accept without question a path laid out for us, the dimensions of everything change and we begin to view ourselves in a different light. Suddenly the eyes of passersby are raised from off the ground and a common bond develops, and people begin to gather and understand that they are one at heart. Suddenly, we are content to drift with the tide of humanity and events like a wave that has reached its shore. Some of us have traveled this far only to get lost within the crowd or within ourselves, instead of strengthening our resolve to remain on course and be our true selves.

The philosophers and agents from the philosophy of opposites canvas more aggressively here in Winter than at the other three rest stops. They know that we are seasoned veterans who have ignored and probably refuted them before. This is their last resort at total persuasion against the convictions of the spirit. This emphasis on belief is part of the strategy to induct us into the notion that there is, or can be, something spiritual about the material. We can overemphasize the importance of very mundane, material things to the extent where they have us attaching spiritual meanings to them and creating ceremonies around them as if our lives or lifestyles depend on them.

At the Winter rest stop, here there are icicle treats that bring you happiness and love, and drinks that make you radiate with youth and promises of a long and fruitful life. You can adopt sisters and brothers with a common cause and begin to be inducted into your own hall of fame. That genuine appeal to our emotional need is the transition to this bifocal state of mind that can overwhelm us into becoming a part of this grand illusion. There are entrapments of the spirit that can ambush us as clandestinely on the inside as much as the outside.

TRAVELLING BY INTUITION

Changing faces and places give predators the added advantage of appearing to reduce the real threat of their true intentions. They can pretend they are one of us and put up quite a convincing act. The human mind wants to conform to what other humans do, so that the parade of conformists filing towards our direction is not as genuine as they seem. They are headhunters from the philosophy of opposites putting up an act to win us over as a trophy to their cause.

Jerry S. Barry

When we find ourselves suddenly popular, where our solitude is suddenly punctured for reasons unknown to us, that is when we should realize that even the Winter rest stop is programmed for our reception and accommodation. The lack of incentive we felt in the beginning was our intuition from the spirit that is preparing our subconscious for the onslaught of hypocrisy and deceit that will pervade the atmosphere at this crucial stopover.

For most people traveling in winter, the safety and security of the rest stop are ideal reasons to postpone the journey and satisfy the creature comforts for the while. When too many travelers swarm around us like bees attending their queen, our intuition should have given us the alert that such circumstances are not in our better favor.

Our intuition is not only the alert mechanism that captures thoughts and intentions like bubbles in the atmosphere, but it is also the switch that connects us to the universal power grid to sustain our spiritual being. It alerts us when we are getting disconnected from our energy source and losing touch with ourselves.

We do not go on a journey to make stops, although we do make stops during a journey. We have had enough experience in dealing with rest stops and the weather conditions in any season, including Winter, that we should know not to make this stop an exception. While it is true that when conditions change we should change ourselves to suit those conditions, that refers mainly to the physical or material but not the spiritual. The only spiritual conditions that change are the ones that result when we disconnect to compromise with the material. That is how we get involved with or even addicted to all manners of popular culture that try to bridge the gap with substitutions and forgeries.

Life is a journey that has to be lived fully so that the very essence of our existence is projected to the life source to which it connects. Making stops is incidental and often consequential, but they are not an integral part of any journey. Stops are for speculation and taking stock of the rudimentary of the journey, not to surrender all the gains of a journey to satisfy the demands of a stop. If we do not get our priorities right, our system can grow cold and freeze our ignition, making it difficult to ever get started again.

When people complain about the weather, it could be a sign that their ignition has frozen in their system and they have lost their connection to the higher realms of their consciousness, and now lack the confidence to exist, much less function, on any level.

The journey of life is equivalent to a battle of endurance and strength, and those that fall by the wayside get trapped in rest stops to pursue a ghostlike existence.

MAINTAINING OUR FOCUS IN WINTER

When we are on a mission, we should know exactly why we have stopped at a rest stop. When we lose touch with our mission, we feel compelled to stop to find ourselves and our way again. That is how and when we get consumed by the rudiments and circumstances of the rest stop. We shape our journey by the way we think and act.

Our thoughts send out concrete messages through the atmosphere that influence the kinds of experiences we have or will have. What we think is what we are and is how the world relates to us. When we limit ourselves to stops and incidentals, the events that clutter our lives become petty squabbles and intrigues, punctuated by little treats of pleasure similar to what we are likely to encounter at a rest stop in a bar.

In Winter, our appetite can be increased to consume small pleasures and excitements in order to offset the dreary outlook of the winter atmosphere. The hunger within us that creates the need for petty pleasures and excitements are not the products of the spirit, but the result of a compromise that has been reached deep in the subconscious mind to question the high ideals of the spirit. That is when we acquiesce to lower ethics and behavior.

The hazards of the rest stop are equally challenging as those we encounter along the roadway. The dangers on the outside cannot be compared to those manufactured on the inside. There is no greater fear than those that arise from illusions projected from our minds, the phobias of our greatest disappointments and apprehensions in life.

There are the illusions we create around the things we choose to believe as we strive to make them a reality. There is the Pygmalion effect of forcing people to become what we make them out to be to suit our warped expectations, and they often choose not to disappoint us. They do it with passion and resolve to surprise themselves, and us.

Severe potholes in our thinking revive the phantoms of the poverty of the spirit. They take on a life and personality of their own to follow us everywhere we go. There are persons and systems that produce phobias, like getting us to dislike ourselves for who and what we are, and to ignore our better qualities and the musings of our own spirit.

A system of self-destruction is the most effective. It

establishes this degenerate outlook of ourselves as the ultimate standard to work for and emulate in our lives, and serves as a model for the next generation. It feeds us with destructive propaganda that insults our culture, our people, our dreams and aspirations. It is a system that pervades our schooling, our recreation and entertainment, and filters even into our religious beliefs.

We can undo those illusions by first upgrading them to be as real as we want them to be. We can give them life to motivate ourselves into viewing them for what they really are, then we can convert them into a game for our entertainment. Illusions can be destructive when they overwhelm, overpower and confuse us, but they can also be the rainbow of our lives when we are able to utilize their energy to recharge our system.

We can convert the disappointments
of our lives into a process for
enjoyment to guide and entertain,
enlightening other travelers that are
inflicted with the disease.

We can make our misfortune into a medicine for the world. The potency of our medicine is the truth and sincerity with which we tell it, the tools with which we interpret it, and the precision with which we apply it. How we choose to analyze our experience and the world in general determines how we are going to exist within it. We are no better off in the rest stop than on the highway if we can hardly distinguish between illusion and reality and how to address them within their proper context.

Not all ghosts and demons are figments of our imagination. Some are really the companions and celebrities of our own thoughts and philosophies that give closure to our intentions and aspirations. They stand alert within and around us to see, hear and speak for us, through us and the intrigues that we secretly harbor in the backs of our minds. The secret passions that we are unable to control are the zombies that accompany us day and night, waiting for circumstances and events to lure us into revealing our true allegiance, for what we do not want to show ourselves to be.

How can we travel where we are supposed to go when our heart is focused on going somewhere else, enjoying one lane and traveling on another?

Obviously, driving without due care and attention is a perfect recipe for an accident. Yet accidents do not just happen by themselves. Zombies do not follow us because they are lost or have been misguided. They are attracted to that part of us that nurtures their world, that link to the underworld of our dark intentions that we cover up in the daytime.

Zombies do not follow us because they are lost

How can we see potholes in front of us when we are busy looking everywhere else? The germs of a bad idea or intent always seek an outlet to flourish and grow, going through the same ritual or process as a good idea or intent. Everything strives to be productive, whether for the positive or the negative and each also generate its own energy or enthusiasm. Such is also the nature of illusions which can be very bipolar, equally obsessed with both sides of itself.

So, whether we are inside, at the rest stop, or outside on the highways of life, how we drive to navigate the circumstances of life would depend on our vision and the perspective from which we choose to look. Being inside at the rest stop brings us closer into contact with circumstances that reveal the bipolar nature of the world in which we live.

THE BIPOLAR NATURE OF THE LIFE WE LIVE

The world begins from within us and from what we choose to believe. We start with a belief until it grows into a resolution, and in time it becomes our dream and total aspiration. Very soon we are working at a level of aspiration and forget that this all started as a belief or piece of wishful thinking. The things we choose to believe can become real, taking a life and form of their own according to our specifications. Their capacities are no greater than our will or deficiencies. They are energized by the power we invest in them, if we are ever able to become aware of that.

Everything in our world connects to us according to our belief and how we view ourselves within the context of that belief. A peasant may view his lowly cottage as a palace surrounded by a garden of paradise. The constraints of poverty and social class may not impact him as it should since he has not yet experienced in his mind what it means to be poor. This is why he gets confused when the frivolities of modern living invade the world around him in the form of luxury cars and other technological inventions.

Symbols of money and possession reflected in gold, dollars, and the prestige that go with them do not penetrate or influence him emotionally, since they do not affect him internally. To get his attention, we will have to radically change his external surroundings to uproot the customary interactions he has with his natural environment. Even so, his confidence in himself and his world is so concrete, that any interjection of values to any part of it would be an imposition.

People who view their world from the inside develop a natural rhythm to interact with their environment to the extent where they do not burden themselves attaching material value to their experiences. When we attach values to certain items or events around us, embellishing them with symbols and meanings, we impose such values upon our subconscious to alter the way our spirit works. With the spirit there are no value systems that categorize anything or anyone.

The spirit responds to everyone and everything from the window of a firm conviction that everything serves a purpose and we exist to serve our purpose in relation to it. The spirit is preoccupied with service and purpose, the embellishment of the moment for its own sake. When we attach our mediocre system of values, we contaminate the process that the spirit employs to provide us with the balance we desperately need to bring enrichment to our lives. How we view ourselves within the context of our world invariably determines how we function within it.

To view ourselves within the context of an external value system based on material things is to make ourselves subservient to the things we value, thereby regulating our philosophy, our actions and decisions in life based on those values we adopt. We need to value ourselves from the universality of our existence and not from within the enclaves of ethnicity, race, cultural or religious orientation.

Very often we unconsciously lock ourselves into these cubicles that only provide us with a limited understanding of who we really are. This produces a limited understanding of the world around us and the relationship we have to our environment. Looking out from cubicles, we can only perceive within the limitations of those cubicles, where our sense of purpose becomes confined to the dynamics of the philosophy of the cubicle we embrace.

For those who embrace this kind of outlook or philosophy, there is a kind of wisdom based on the lack of understanding. This wisdom makes itself self-assuring and convincing enough for some people to stoically believe in and defend. They believe that they are right even when they are not knowledgeable enough about what is right for them.

If there is a value system we must employ, it is the one that awakens us to the importance of our existence in shaping the present and in influencing the forces around us that depend on our contribution as much as they contribute to our benefit. When we live life purely because of what we can get out of it, we devalue the benefits of our very existence and every other factor that interacts with us.

The philosophy we hold about our existence and sense of purpose is what determines the lane we choose in our travels in this life and how we socialize at our Winter rest stop. We exist within the time and place that is relative to our purpose in our life's journey. Other travelers at the rest stop become reflections of ourselves at the cross section of our journey. When we meet with them on the basis of the spirit, we need not say a word because of a perfect understanding that we share instantly. When we pass each other at the rest stop it is not because of lack of acquaintance, but because we are focused on the urgency of where we are headed.

STRAGGLERS

What is more important to those of us imbued with the spirit is the journey itself and the validity of life at the moment. This validity is what binds us together on the same mission on the same journey, when we share the bond of the spirit. There are no peripheries or trivialities to consider along the way to dissuade us from our sense of urgency, not even the luring comforts of the rest stop can slow us down into complacency. Stragglers with a common interest gather into cubicles to entertain themselves, plunder and loot from an assortment of possibilities when all of human destinies meet at a major junction. They scramble to beat the lights to get ahead of everybody else, to gain every possible advantage and exploit every weakness within their grasp. The roving noises of the rest stop are not without pain, anger, frustration and shame. Within this crowd of revelers are the strong devouring the weak, yet they all revel together because they each function within the cubicle of their addiction.

This journey of life for stragglers is a series of sleepovers where they make one excuse after another for not getting ahead on the real journey of their lives, sacrificing their true mission for ill-gotten pleasure and gains. This rest stop has become the one where they intend to fulfill their base desires and vernacular intents they had harbored along the way. They become consumed with the glut of the exotic, the erotic and the extreme, and advance every logic to justify staying at this rest stop. Their sense of urgency has been confined to the material, to grasp as much out of circumstances as they can to extract profit and benefits for themselves at the expense of others.

The maddening crowd may appear to be revelers enjoying life when in fact there is a vicious struggle for survival under the false pretense of camaraderie. Lack of integrity is contagious among the throng of stragglers that huddle close together to hide their low intentions from one another. They hover under the shelter of partnership, marriage, an organization or a cult to show how generous they can be. They are at the forefront of the ceremony adorned with all the regalia and pomp of vanity, but their masks are tightly fitted to their faces to make them look real. They are just an illusion of themselves and they do not know it.

They have deceived themselves for so long, that they have come to believe in assumptions as reality. Stragglers who have lost hope grasp at assumptions to fill the void in their lives. They create a parallel reality like a religion to satisfy that yearning and follow its precepts. They adopt heroes and stars of pop culture and induct them into their hall of fame so that they can invest into them the powers they want them to have. Clubs and societies are irresistible for them, so deep are their yearnings to belong to something big and secure.

It all started with a belief designed to circumvent the truth, and it builds on airs of expectations that seem to resemble the truth. Such substitute ingredients are created for the appetite of fools who assume they can cheat their way through life by taking the low service road. They want to settle for less to gain more. They settle for imitations and fakes and want to cash in on the same higher value they had not worked originally to achieve.

Agents of the philosophy of opposites are busier at the Winter rest stop as they are organizing cubicles like stalls to accommodate the lost and the misguided. This allows stragglers to continue to feel comfortable in their dilemma and resort to the next level of denial. Higher doses of indoctrination will nullify the pain and also neutralize their capacity to redeem themselves ever. The deeper they go into the woods of false assurance, the less they will have left of their self-esteem to find their way back out.

A person who has lost his self-esteem becomes a ghost unto his own self, scaring his true self at every turn. The worst torture is the kind we inflict upon ourselves, when storms and tempests rage within as peace and tranquility exists without. The cubicles that are so crowded are really holding pens for those plagued by regret and self-indulged addiction.

We who are driven by the spirit appear to become zombies in their mind's eye. When the mind is distorted or disturbed, it sees through a distorted lens and behold nothing but distortion, regardless of what object is within its view. Even when it knows elements of the truth and is presented with them, the mind of the distorted will seek to fulfill its expectations and deny the truth. That is how we imprison ourselves in a world of our own making, making illusions of material and social aggrandizements into the masters that control our destiny. We become caged pets of these monsters that prey upon our secret desires and aspirations, leading us into derelict pastures of doubt and hopelessness. No wonder so many stragglers wander around at the Winter rest stop, inflicted with the fear of continuing the journey they had so confidently begun.

HOW TRAVELERS BECOME STRAGGLERS

The wholesale demoralization that occurs among stragglers before our very eyes is not accidental and we should avoid the pitfall of misreading it. Firstly, stragglers are in that unfortunate situation because they had not focused on the journey, only on themselves. It seems logical, practical and even natural to make ourselves and our needs the first priorities of any venture. Therein lies the paradox into which the vast majority of us get entrapped.

The most persuasive lines from the philosophy of opposites would reinforce that theory forthwith to appeal to our egocentric desires and motives. That is like trying to fill a bottomless pit. People who are full of aspirations with priorities involving material things are never satisfied. Actually, they become greedier, wanting more, envious towards those who are getting more, and vicious in the games of business and politics to take as much as possible from those naïve enough to trust them. Once we are locked into the material side of life, our perspective and the decisions we make conform easily to the principles of the philosophy of opposites.

That is why, after three seasons that should have nurtured us to be valuable veterans on the highways of life, we settle for picking up leftover pennies on the roadway and cheap entertainment at the rest stops. We keep wanting more and more of what we think we are getting. That is why stragglers are stricken with complacency at the rest stop and convince themselves that they have 'arrived'. They view the peripheries and extensions of ordinary living as a primary substance of the purpose of life. They get preoccupied with the pageants and parades, rituals and routines that add to the grand circus at the Winter rest stop.

People who are engaged with the spiritual level on their journey in life do not put their valuable mission on hold for trinkets and cheap entertainment. Life has no down time or absentee time. It is a fatal mistake to utilize the virtues of the spirit to pursue the benefits and rewards of the selfish pursuits.

HYPOCRITES

There are always a few among us who try playing the double game of posturing in the spirit but living in the flesh. There will always be those who think they can cheat with the spirit. They are among the maddening crowd busying themselves at the Winter rest stop, chasing after the shadows of themselves to find a way out of the prison in their minds. They have even lost their sense of direction to where the highway is. They spend their moments in perpetual melodrama putting up a façade or acts of diversion to feed their self-denial. A life of regret plagued with perambulations and false pretenses is not worth living, especially when it is conducted at the cost of the betrayal of the spirit. However, life can be very forgiving when we can bring our minds to the point of forgiving ourselves and others.

In the highway of life we travel the path of the tangible and material, events and circumstances toward the higher realm of perfection and enlightenment. Our every encounter is wired with the symbols of truth in all their manifestations. Whether we recognize them or not depends on the manner in which we travel, the lane we choose and our level of consciousness that keeps us alert to the showers of the gifts of life around us.

Our accomplishments in the journey we take are not measured by the virtue of the distance we have covered but by the virtue of our composure and wisdom through the gifts we bring and the light we radiate for all humanity.

We are not in this journey of life for ourselves alone. The world neither spins to focus on us, nor do we have the power or authority to spin the world to suit our every whim and fancy. We are merely a part of a series of coordinated sources of energy that build to a climax according to the laws of nature.

THE UNIVERSAL WILL VERSUS PHYSICAL POWER

At another level the spirit is driven by the power of universal thought and moves in the direction of will to the realm of upliftment and truth. Neither one is within our control. We are that infinitesimal bearing that helps the smooth turning of this giant chain of circumstances that create the history we make today. That bearing can choose not to be there, and the world would still function either with a substitute or missing link.

We should never underestimate the power of the universal will that governs the spirit merely because it associates itself with humble interactions with mankind. We should not question its legitimacy or integrity just because it is unseen and can hardly be measured in tangible ways. It is natural to want to relate to something by comparing it to something we have come to know from experience, but it is also not unusual to live an entire life interacting in the wrong way with something or someone we had never really come to know.

We can assure ourselves that we have really had an experience when we are in complete control and understand the dynamics of that experience. We tend to choose to invest ourselves in and around the forces of physical power because they are connected in many ways to our basic needs and our survival. Physical power in the human psyche is almost never connected to anything uplifting except for the aggrandizement of the self. Hence it involves some system, machinery or strategy to subdue, exploit, restrict and even destroy someone else. It is generally a resolution to invoke the dark side of our nature to impose or exercise control for personal or political gain.

Physical power can consume us into a circular entrapment of logical thinking that we are doing something uplifting. Once we have persuaded ourselves that we are on a mission, there is no depth to which we would lower ourselves to commit acts of cruelty or immorality to satisfy our appetites.

Our attachment or affiliation to circles of power that operate within our local environment can force us to yield or adopt that power source as the foundation towards the fulfillment of our aspiration.

Physical power requires the fuel of compliance and unquestionable obedience to support the engine on that grid of power under the prevailing circumstances. Nature in its pure state has no use for it, since nature already operates within the realms of its own fulfillment and requires nothing for itself. Whatever it gets, it schedules to be given to support the cycle of life patterns on which it depends.

THE FUTILITY OF SELF-AGGRANDIZEMENT

Imagine how the birds and insects extract their benefits from nature while still serving the function of reproduction and pollination. Nature itself demonstrates ways in which living things synchronize their needs and their functions among themselves to coexist in a harmonious relationship we have come to appreciate and take for granted. Yet, with all our intellectual superiority, pronounced civility and social organization, we have not been able to achieve that level of harmony and synchronization of functions to create a better and more peaceful world for ourselves. Among us humans, there is always an overtone of the forceful imposition or interjection of power of some sort, feeding into some system of corruption or exploitation for the benefit of a few people.

Nothing seems to persuade us from giving up this machinery of egocentricity to save our species from the plague of wars and systems of oppression and corruption that we have come to accept as normal, or even necessary. It seems as though the potholes and ditches are for us a compulsory process of travel in life, and no proliferation of great ideas can deter us from clinging tenaciously to the legacies of our tumultuous past. It seems like having something to cry about must be engrained into our aspirations individually and as a species.

Perhaps we need these as appetizers to help us to focus on great ideas, as if the struggles of life itself do not present valuable ideas of their own. We are never short of great ideas in all our interactions as civilized human beings; it is just that we tend to select and implement those that recycle our problems, instead of solving them. Somehow it becomes pertinent and relevant to maintain a little discrimination here, inject a little racism there, exchange a little peace for a few petty conflicts, or most of all, reverse all the gains of our human intelligence to maintain a lopsided balance of good and evil.

We are in the habit of not acknowledging great ideas that can work towards a solution to our human problems, even when those ideas come from our religion or educational training. Instead of harvesting these ideas from the products and processes of our technological advancement, we persist in being selective for the wrong reasons to advance the wrong purposes.

When we find ourselves in the depth of darkness off track into the woods and the critters begin to stalk us, we tend to do better in writing manuals of history and speeches of repentance more so to consolidate our actions than to question or reject them. This is why the rest stop in the Winter journey of our lives will always serve different purposes for different people. Instead of enjoying a pause for leisure and pure entertainment, we may spend precious golden hours reliving phobias and reviving demons of our past, to reinterpret circumstances and situations that have plagued us with remorse or regret. No wonder we can get distracted by the neon lights and human enclaves gathered at the rest stop.

We may be looking for ways to soothe our inner burnings and fulfill our deepest yearnings and blame it on the rest stop. We may be seeking an organization or clique of persons that best reflect our views and aspirations. All others become ghosts and demons who transform into critters once we exit the highways. Some of us bring an end to our journey because we have no sound reason to continue. We are exactly trapped or delayed at the rest stop: we have nowhere else to go.

There are some of those among us who have traveled all the way through three seasons and still do not know where we are going. There are those who inculcate high ambitions of where they want to go but do not want to undertake the responsibilities of taking themselves there. No wonder the prospects of being at the rest stop can present such a dilemma. Some of us are so far removed from the reality of our lives that we tend to picture ourselves in grand illusions moving on while we are actually standing still. Without realizing it, the agenda we have for our lives are invested in the power structures of the system to which we have endeared ourselves.

Power structures tend to create dead ends that organize their catch according to their level of helplessness so that they can be processed efficiently and effectively. Much of what goes on at the rest stop in the wintry journey of our lives had long been programmed into us before we got there.

Jerry S. Barry

Those of us who have matured with travel know when it is time to take the exit onto the highway of fulfillment

EXIT FROM THE WINTER REST STOP

It is possible for some of us to get too comfortable with our compromises and addictions, so that we may abandon our journey and permanently stay at the rest stop. For some, the journey itself has been too challenging to even start; so, they stayed behind since Spring, dreaming that providence would pamper them forever. Time has moved away and left them behind and they interpret and relate to everything out of turn and out of context. They assume that they had cheated on life and won, but nobody is there to help them celebrate because everyone else has moved on and left them behind.

However, those of us who have matured with travel know when it is time to move on and take the exit onto the highway of fulfillment and discovery. It is fulfillment because of our enthusiasm to move to the next plane of inquiry and consciousness, when life will bring us new inspirations according to our gifts. It is discovery because we will see ourselves transformed with a unique vision of life and living among our fellow men. We who travel the journey of life with solemn introspection know that the pursuit of perfection and self-refinement never really ends.

For those of us to whom the milestones of the journey of life are merely markers for decisions we are required to make, there could hardly be any beginning. When a mission is ours, we act to fulfill it with deep resolve and conviction because it pervades everything we do, think and feel. Some of us come to that realization very early in our travels, since the beginning of Spring, and others later along the way. It is that awakening that arrests our very nature to stay and sustains us throughout the journey.

A mission is more deeply engrained into our system beyond the level of belief or persuasion, and its fulfillment becomes a reward in itself. We become the journey and the journey becomes us. Resolutions and missions are great propositions and worthy intentions, but the greatest promise we can make is that which we make to ourselves, provided we are equally committed to keeping it. What we do in our travel is cross borders into new dimensions of truth, up over hills into new levels of understanding.

Although the routines of negotiating circumstances and events are mostly physical, the borders and plains that we traverse are spiritual, refining our purpose and conviction every moment along the way. This is how our engagements towards the fulfillment of our mission or conviction become our inherent gifts or rewards. When we are sincere about our mission and dedicated in our actions, we become the wellspring of our own rewards, like a magic pool or fountain that replenishes itself with richness and lusters of light.

There is a connection between heaven and earth as much as there is a connection between body and the spirit. What we know in the mind as enlightened by the spirit will not shower down to us in gifts and blessings unless we translate them into actions and firm decisions.

The engine that moves a mission is powered by firm actions, not intentions. The will that engages the mind and mobilizes the body shifts gears to the realm of the spirit and we become self-sufficient in our driving - over valleys, hills and open plains. When we become the very reflection of our mission, driving becomes routine and involuntary, regardless of the gravel or rocks on the road, or the nature of the terrain. The horizon unfolds behind the light before us, to reveal the fields and orchards of a harvest of bountiful wisdom and joy.

The rest stop that we have left behind us is no longer necessary or relevant to our travel at this stage. When our body and mind have achieved the rhythm enough to synchronize with the spirit, we generate all those comforts and conveniences of a rest stop within ourselves.

WHAT WINTER TRAVEL MEANS

We become the world in which we choose to live, and that is the world which unfolds that we end up living. Each milestone that marks our decision in the lane that we travel helps to shape the destination of the journey that we take. We may have acted impulsively in the beginning due to our anxiety to discover ourselves. Even the lanes in which we may have traveled might have come upon us incidentally due to our lack of experience and foresight.

Now that we are veteran travelers in the Winter of our lives, we have outgrown the privilege of excusing ourselves for riding into ditches and potholes. It is while traveling that we come to a real understanding of what the journey of life is all about and that our view of life becomes the very equivalent of how we live it. The borders that we cross have more to do with the levels of our understanding and how we are able to incorporate these into our daily living.

Heaven and earth are just as relative as thought and action, but the action that results in the fulfillment of our highest aspirations must be determined by thoughts enriched and enlightened by a refined spirit. When the physical is not dictated and controlled by the mental and spiritual, we find ourselves perambulating within the limitations of physical desires and abilities and the social aggrandizements that accompany them. This tendency lends itself to excessive boasting, attachments to grand illusions and a strict adherence to rituals and ceremonies that leave only tangible evidence of accomplishments. It is this dedication to the tangible that represents our choice or focus in life and the nature of the journey that we make. People at this level of understanding like to show tangible material substance of what they have achieved in life.

Our obsession with the tangible relics of the physical may belabor our minds with decisions and actions that could alter the nature and quality of our journey. Our concept of insurance in life may therefore be grounded in monetary savings and earnings from investments, the outward display of affection from family and friends and a long menu of personal pleasures. There is a big difference between building our insurance in life based on our assurance of what we can get out of it and our dedication of what we want to give to it. Tangible assets are nothing short of grand illusions, regardless of the value of their physical presence.

Not only do they tease us with their false pretenses, but they are also a magnet for a whole string of aggressive predators. We find ourselves viciously competing for what is ours against usurpers that can be counted even among our family members, friends, and close acquaintances. The physical and material always tend to glitter, for all the wrong reasons, imposing unnecessary wear and tear on our vehicle in the course of travel.

What should have been an assurance for our peace and safety turns out to be a heavy liability that keeps our minds fixed downwards on the lookout for potholes and unexpected surprises. A life built around material gains and possessions and driven by grammarian logic would breed its own regrets, vendettas, revenge, and entrapments that dramatically alter the way our life is lived. When these peripheries of life divert us from our real nature and the journey that we take, we tend to miss the significance of the experiences we have and interpret events and circumstances in ways that are confined within those peripheries.

If our journey is measured by how much we have accumulated, then our preoccupation with accommodating such gains would certainly prevent us from enjoying them. The things in life that have all the characteristics and qualities of being tangible may not be as tangible as they may appear. Even the values for them are so sketchy and unstable, their true meaning and purpose in life melt like ice or butter in the light of circumstances and events that require their attention. In the material world focused on greed and power, such tangibles are a primary target, and so are their owners.

The system generated by the philosophy of opposites is aimed at devouring all assets and persons to support its machinery of excess, and will not spare any morsel that is within its reach. Like having a million dollars to spend in a betting shop, we begin with the confidence of what we think we have, not realizing that we are gambling our assets away with every decision we make and every action we take.

It is the intangible that makes itself tangible in the real journey of life. The intangible focuses on the journey that correlates with the one we take within our minds, the one dictated and generated by the spirit. The journey within is the one that makes the physical and material journey meaningful. This is where the predators from the philosophy of opposites would really like to prowl to sell us their concepts of heaven and happiness. They never stop trying, although they do not have the means or the tools, or even a comparative product. Their idea of inwardness or the spirit condescends to the material and the social in ways that lack depth and understanding.

A journey of inwardness, governed by the spirit, needs no ritual or ceremony to be initiated, has no limit to the height to which it can aspire, and needs none of the physical or material to reinforce itself and its principles. The spirit is the engine that dictates the pace of travel, whether uphill or down, across one border after another beyond the possible, as far as the eye can see. The ethers of the atmosphere become linked with the light, as the infinite landscape keeps unfolding like the pages of a book. Against a kaleidoscope of light and color, the unsolvable becomes solved and the impossible becomes possible, as we stand at the bottom of the stairway spiraling up into a tornado of light.

BEYOND THE HORIZON

Life is not worth the living
Unless we have truly lived it.
The Journey was not worth the traveling
Unless we have come to love it.
Love and life are true partners of the spirit
Who must get married along the way
When meaning blends with purpose
In the things we do and say.
Life is lived through the channels
Of the messages that we send.
The patterns of the path of love
Pave our way right to the end.
Both partners will then fuse together
For the real journey they must take,
One for life and one for love
And both for goodness sake.

Jerry S. Barry

THE CONCLUSION:

CLUES TO THE SYMBOLS OF TRAVEL

Everybody is on a journey, whether we choose to travel or not. If we obstinately refuse to travel, life and time will place us on a platform and take us through the motions of our journey to the end. The vehicle on which we travel is our knowledge-based understanding. The highway is our chronological, physical, and emotional growth combined. We drive through motivation by what we are able to see. It is the fuel that moves the engine of our faculties. Our spiritual intuition gives us the insight to see beyond the windscreen of issues and circumstances, while our philosophical orientations influence our decision making. The rest stop is the respite or introspective phase in our growth when we reflect and respond to physical and mental growth and spiritual maturity. Our memory, history, and ancestry are reflected in our rear-view mirrors.

THE CHALLENGE

If ever you decide to live this life, life it fully and not partially. Respond with your whole being as deeply and sincerely as you can. In all your travels and deliberations, however, observe the speed limit and not become reckless with self-confidence. Be prepared to stop, when you must, on the highway when you travel and the rest stop when you are tired. You must be very wary of hallucination; if, and when you are lucky to recognize that you are having one, it is a sign that you have over extended yourself. While on your way, recognize your fellow travelers but be cautious not to acknowledge some of them for who they really are. You may regret it. That is their secret comfort and convenient escape from themselves. Tell them what they want to hear if you know what that is. If you do not know, try not to assume or imagine. Just smile and remain silent.

In as many ways as you can, learn to enjoy your travel. You will never be able to travel that road again. Relish each moment in ways you can design for yourself. You will need a partner to help you see yourself and where you are going. A good partner is your co-pilot and a perfect reflection of you. By submerging yourself in somebody else, you discover yourself better. Learn to be fully alert so that you do not fall asleep at the wheel. Know your destination before you set out to travel. Prepare in as many ways as you can. Acquire all that you need, but with more skills and foresight than resources. Never mind the bumps and occasional noise of gravel on the road: they are a part of travel, but make bountiful uses of your rear-view mirrors.

You do not experience life just by being alive and in it. You have to first respond to the challenges of life to even begin to experience it.

When you respond and begin to experience life in your own way, then you truly begin to live it. You may read all you want about life and gain more experience in reading about it. Your responding to the challenges of life, however, requires skill, decisiveness, flexibility, and commitment to moral principles. Each one of us was born with that obligation to commit to the path of the perfection of our body and spirit. We have no choice but to go forward. What we choose to do as we go forward is our right and privilege. You may choose to engage in the philosophy of Opposites but it's fatal to reverse on the highway of life.

Be very careful of cheap readymade theories and fashionable ways of thinking being fabricated to make you feel good and self-fulfilled. They may not concern you and are designed to prey upon your limitations to confuse you. Consult with your rear-view mirror. Know who you are, from where you came, and where you are going. Look straight ahead for yourself and remember that this journey you are on prepares you for the other one that lies ahead.

Jerry S. Barry

THE PARADOX OF LIFE IS THE SHAPE YOU GIVE TO IT

Life never gives you anything, unless you dedicate your life to it. You have within you the potential to bless and to curse. You manifest your power in the manner you do things, the way you think and the things you do. You are so much as you think you are and no more. Use your power to shape the life you live, or the life you are forced to live will shape you. Life is a challenge not because of what it does with you, but because of what you do with it.

LIFE'S LIVING QUESTIONS

Did you ever examine the life you are living
to make sure you are alive in it?
Do you make note of the manner in which you
are travelling if you can avoid a ditch or a pit?
Are you your captain, in charge of the rudder
or the driver at the steering wheel?
Can you see clearly what is in the horizon,
limiting what you do to what you feel?
Are you paying rapt attention or are you just
sleeping wide awake at the wheel?

How can it be fun to endure making a journey
and you do not know where it is you are
going?
How much fun can there be to get bigger
when there is so much pain in growing?
How much progress can you make travelling
when your vehicle is struck?
What beauty can you discern in the world
around you when you are tangled among a
whole ton of muck?
How can you keep searching for something
you can hardly identify?
Why are you so obsessed with seeking the
truth when you are so busy living a lie?

How can you be so sure you know where you
are going

When you have no idea where you are coming
from?
How can you begin to relate to that which is
weak when you were never exposed to that
which is strong?
When you have no clue to that which is right,
how can you stand up to oppose that which is
wrong?

When your convictions are so very flimsy
and the head you are using so light,
What will be the source of your strength
when you stand to put up a fight?
How can you insist it is you who made the
decision when you are so busy following the
trend?
Why do you say you resolve to do better
and still stay in the rut to the end?
How can you sail to the middle of the ocean
and be so callous as to abandon your ship?
Is it the obligations of travel
or the weight of the cargo that forced you to
abandon it?
Do you still wish you had done better with
your life compared to what you had done
before?
Have you made one single step to fulfill that
wish or are you still making promises galore?

ABOUT THE AUTHOR

Jerry S. Barry, artist and art educator, poet and writer, has always taken a keen interest in philosophy and religion to explore the mysteries of life and living. Through his paintings and poetry, he has explored a wide varieties of issues based on the common theme of life. Throughout his career of over four decades as a teacher and educator, he has had the kinds of experiences with families and communities to keep alive the pastoral tendencies he displayed as a child. His strong figurative writing are influences from his art and poetry out of which the ideas for this book emerged.

Mr. Barry has a Bachelors in Art Education from Illinois State University, a Masters in Special Education from Long Island University and a Master of Fine Arts in Painting from the University of Hartford. He is also the author of the book: *A Letter to my Prodigal Son.*

Book cover illustrated by the author

Visit his website: www.bluesakie.com

Jerry S. Barry